THE
BIBLE TO-DAY

THE
BIBLE TO-DAY

BY

C. H. DODD

*Norris-Hulse Professor of Divinity in the
University of Cambridge*

CAMBRIDGE
AT THE UNIVERSITY PRESS
1946

Printed in Great Britain at the University Press, Cambridge
(Brooke Crutchley, University Printer)
and published by the Cambridge University Press
Cambridge, and Bentley House, London
Agents for U.S.A., Canada, and India: Macmillan

IN PIAM MEMORIAM

JOHANNIS MARTINI CREED

CONLEGAE ET AMICI

CONTENTS

PREFACE

THIS BOOK represents a course of 'open lectures' given under the auspices of the Divinity Faculty of the University of Cambridge. The text is partly based on shorthand notes taken by hearers of the lectures, among whom I am particularly indebted to Miss M. Buchanan. Both the substance of the lectures and the general arrangement and manner of treatment are preserved, at the cost of some repetition, but the material has undergone a measure of revision.

Quotations from the Old and New Testaments usually follow the Revised Version, but not scrupulously. I have sometimes silently altered it, and sometimes made my own translation.

C. H. D.

Cambridge, October 1945

CHAPTER I

THE BIBLE: WHAT IT IS

WHAT is the Bible?

An obvious answer would be that it is the sacred book of the Christian religion (and, in part, of Judaism), as the Koran is the sacred book of Islam, or the Vedas sacred books of Hinduism. If we were finding a place for it in a well-arranged library, we might put it on a shelf labelled 'Sacred Books'. So far, so good. But the term 'sacred' is too vague to tell us much about the Bible, and in fact the suggested parallel with the Koran and the Vedas is far from exact.

From another point of view, the Bible is not a book, but a collection of books commonly bound up between the same covers. Among these books there is a great variety, both in form and in contents. There is prose narrative, both historical and fictitious; there are legal codes; there are proverbs and moral maxims; there is even personal correspondence. Again there is lyrical and dramatic poetry; there is the peculiar *genre* of literature which can only be described as 'prophetical'; and there is liturgical literature, designed expressly for use in public worship. This list suggests, but does not exhaust, the range of variety.

If, therefore, we are to place the Bible appropriately on the shelves of our library, we might have to arrange different parts under different headings. Some of these would not be noticeably religious. There are large sections of the biblical literature which reflect the ordinary secular interests of mankind. In some of the greatest historical narratives of the Bible the specifically religious element is quite in the background and the secular human interest is to the fore; for example, in the moving story of David and Absalom.[1] Again, if we isolate those parts which in our proposed classification would have to be labelled 'Religion', some of them do not appear to have any particular relevance to the religious life as it is understood by civilized men in our contemporary world; such as the detailed regulations for the ritual slaughter of animals in the Book of Leviticus.

But in fact any such dissection of the Bible into its component parts destroys the distinctive flavour which makes it what it is. It is characteristic of this sacred book, or religious literature, that in it the religious element emerges directly out of the crude stuff of human life as it is lived in its many phases; and few of these phases are unrepresented. Whatever may be the religious purport of the Bible, it is to be found in the whole range of the biblical presentation of life, human and secular as it is. Neither 'elegant extracts', nor a selection of texts for 'devotional' reading (though no doubt each may serve a purpose) could convey the rare, indeed the unique, character of the Bible as a body of religious literature.

With all its variety there is after all a real unity in this literature. It is not readily discovered by 'dipping', but forces itself upon the serious and persistent reader. When we begin to search for the principle of unity, the first thing we observe is that the whole of the varied material is strung upon a thread which consists of narrative. This narrative gives a kind of 'cavalcade' of human life through many centuries, beginning in the cloudy realms of myth and legend, and emerging into straightforward history. Upon investigation, it turns out to be the history of a single community, or social group, through many stages of development. The other parts of the Bible relate themselves naturally to this main thread of historical narrative.

1 II Samuel xv–xviii.

Thus a first approach to the unity of the whole is the recognition that the different parts have their origin in the life of a community conscious of a continuous history.

This continuity persists through changes of the most far-reaching kind. When the community first comes into view, it is a Semitic clan, or group of clans, wandering between the two great civilizations centred upon the Euphrates and the Nile. Next it appears as a nation, bearing the national name of 'Israel', settled in its own territory, and governed by its native chieftains and kings. The petty kingdoms decline and fall, and the community ceases to exist as an independent state. With the Babylonian conquest it is absorbed into the all-embracing empire of the Middle East, which under various dynasties persisted through many centuries of the ancient world. Then it reappears in a new form. A small group of returned exiles organizes itself as a partly autonomous community under the suzerainty of the imperial government. The restored community is neither monarchy nor republic. Its rulers are priests. Its legal code is the Law of God. It has its centre in the Temple at Jerusalem with a small amount of contiguous territory, but the writ of its ecclesiastical government runs through hundreds of Jewish colonies, spread over the whole civilized world, and owing political allegiance to various secular states. It is a unique kind of social and political unit, whose actual principle of cohesion is almost entirely religious, though it retains some attachment to a national and geographical centre. In the last phase of all, the national and geographical attachment disappears altogether, and we have the Christian Church. This is a 'catholic' or universal community, transcending all national distinctions in its membership; and yet it is the same community that we have traced all through.

At the very point where the continuity seems decisively broken, where the Old Testament gives place to the New, the continuity of the society is the most emphatically affirmed. It is true that the writers of the New Testament are quite clear that Christianity is a new thing, indeed a 'new creation'[1] of God's hand; and yet it is 'the Israel of God'.[2] They make use of the old historical name. They speak of 'Abraham our father'. 'Our fathers', they say, passed through the Red Sea; received the Law from Moses; tempted God in the wilderness.[3] There is a singularly impressive testimony to this sense of continuity in the eleventh chapter of the Epistle to the Hebrews, where the writer claims not only Moses and the patriarchs, but such splendid savages of a primitive age as Gideon, Samson and Barak, as fellow-members of the 'heavenly Jerusalem',[4] one timeless community running through history but transcending it.

The Church[5] in its worship still preserves this consciousness of continuity. We sing Hebrew Psalms. We read lessons from both Testaments. The language of our prayers is drawn from all parts of the Bible. On Easter Eve, in those churches which follow the traditional Western rite, they sing the hymn called *Exultet*, which commemorates God's dealings with His people in history. 'This is the night in which Thou didst first lead our fathers, the children of Israel, out of Egypt, and didst make them to pass dryshod through the Red Sea.' 'Our fathers': the Church means it seriously. That is part of *our* history. The doings and sufferings of these people are of a piece with our experience within the Church of God at the present day.[6] When in the New Testament the old historic name 'Israel' is applied to this continuous community, it

1 II Corinthians v. 17.   2 Galatians vi. 16.
3 I Corinthians x. 1–11.   4 Hebrews xii. 22–23.
5 'Christ's Holy Catholic Church, that is, the whole congregation of Christian people dispersed throughout the whole world.' This definition (from the 55th Canon of the Church of England) is presupposed throughout this book.
6 See, further, chap. VII, pp. 155 *sqq.*

(4)

means now not any racial or national group, but simply 'the People of God'; that is to say, a community defined solely by its relation to the eternal King of the Universe. It is this conception which in the end gives the Bible its unity.

The Church, then, conceives itself as the continuing embodiment of the historic 'Israel of God'; and we receive the Bible from the hands of the Church. We cannot receive it from anywhere else. If you ask why this particular collection of just these sixty-six books (or eighty, if you count the Apocrypha), and no others, form the unity which is the Bible, the only answer is that these have been handed down by the Church as its 'Scriptures'. These writings have their being, as they had their origin, within the life of a community which traces its descent from Abraham and Moses, from prophets and apostles, and plays its part in the history of our own time; and the Scriptures not only recall its past, but serve the needs of its day-to-day existence in the present.

It is possible to isolate for study one portion or another of these writings. Some have been studied as records of folk-lore, or as documents for the history of primitive culture. Some parts are valuable as sources for oriental history, others for social conditions under the Roman Empire. The modern study of the 'forms' of literature, their origin and early development, has found an exceptionally rich field in the biblical literature, so varied as it is, and extending over so long a period of time. In fact, the several biblical documents are a treasury of materials for scholars in various fields of study. In recent times this specialization has resulted in brilliant illumination of biblical problems from many points of view. But it has also tended to obscure the important fact that the Bible is a definite body of literature, with its own intrinsic unity. Having grown up with the life of a social-religious group, and bearing its stamp all through, it can be adequately understood only in relation to that group-life in its changing phases, including the life of the Christian Church down the centuries and in the present age.

It is a misfortune that in the course of controversy since the Reformation the authority of the Bible has been set over against the authority of the Church, and the Church against the Bible.[1] In reality, the very idea of an authoritative Canon of Scripture is bound up with the idea of the Church.

Let us examine that statement, with the New Testament in view, to begin with. Here we have twenty-seven writings, comprehended under that one title. Why are these particular twenty-seven here? They are not the whole of early Christian literature, by any means. They are a selection out of a larger body of writings, some of which have come down to us, while others were lost, though some of these have been re-discovered by modern archaeologists. It is probable that the impulse to the selection and definition of this particular body of literature was a part of the general impulse towards consolidation which we can trace in the history of the Church in the period after the apostolic age. At that time the continuity of the Church was threatened by extravagances and eccentricities of belief and practice within, as well as by persecution from without. In response to these dangers the Church set out to consolidate its own life and beliefs.[2] Its organs of consolidation were the Rule of Faith (which underlies the historical creeds), the Ministry, and the Canon of Scripture. The term 'canon' means 'norm', or 'standard'. The twenty-seven writings are the norm or standard of Christian faith and life, set forth as such in response to the need for clear definition.

It would, however, be misleading to imagine this process of selection in terms of a panel of experts reviewing a great mass of existing writings, admitting this and excluding that. It is true that some of the minor writings were the subject of long discussion before they were admitted, and in the course of this

1 See chap. ii, pp. 20–23. 2 See chap. iv, pp. 68–69.

discussion some writings which are now outside the New Testament were for a time tentatively admitted into it, but finally rejected. But the important writings, those which give the New Testament its character (about twenty of them), already form a distinct body of literature as soon as we have clear light upon the Church in the second century. Some of the steps by which they came together can be dimly traced; but we can say with confidence no more than this, that the Church intuitively acknowledged the authority of these particular works. It did so quite naturally, because the impulse to select was no different from the impulse that had originally led in various ways to the composition of the works. In the language of the New Testament itself, it was to 'bear witness' to certain central realities that the New Testament writings were first composed, and subsequently compiled into a Canon of Scripture.

The idea which underlies the compilation is well indicated by the title given to the twenty-seven writings. We speak of 'The New Testament', or, more properly, 'The Holy Scriptures of the New Testament'. The word 'testament' here represents an expression which occurs frequently in the Hebrew of the Old Testament and in the Greek of the New. It is usually rendered, in our current versions, by the word 'covenant'. A covenant is a transaction, an agreement or contract between two parties, by which relations between the two are regulated, and by which a certain status is established. The biblical writers, in both main parts of the Canon, speak of a 'covenant' between God and man.[1] In the nature of things, such a covenant cannot be exactly like an agreement on equal terms between man and man. The idea is that God, the eternal King of the Universe, intervenes in human affairs to set up a certain enduring relation of a unique character between Himself and those men who will accept His terms. It is a relation going

1 See chap. III, pp. 39, 41–42, 45–46; chap. IV, pp. 79, 96–97.

beyond that fundamental creaturely relation which all His works necessarily bear to their Creator. The Scriptures of the New Testament, or in other words, the documents of the New Covenant, are the authoritative record of that act of God by which He established relations between Himself and the Church; and they are the charter defining the status of the Church as the people of God, the terms upon which that status is granted, and the obligations it entails.

You will observe that in the attempt to answer the simple question, What is the Bible? (or in particular just now, What is the New Testament?) we have been led inevitably to the profound religious conception of God's 'covenant' with man. We cannot avoid it, if we are to find a definition which expresses its specific character, and assigns the grounds upon which these particular writings were formed into a canon.

Before proceeding further, there is one point which should be made clear. From what has been said, it is clear that the Scriptures of the New Testament grew up within the life of the Church. Their selection out of a larger body of writings was a function of its growing corporate life, in response to a developing situation. Consequently the Church is prior to the Scriptures of the New Testament. On the other hand, the 'covenant' ('testament') itself, that act of God which is attested in the Scriptures, is prior to the Church, for without it there is no Church. This mutual relation between Church and New Testament is fundamental.

To proceed: the 'New Covenant' implies an older covenant with which it stands in contrast. It is as 'The Holy Scriptures of the Old Testament' (covenant) that we receive the thirty-nine books which form the first part of the Canon.

It will be well here to clear up the question of the place of the so-called Apocrypha, those fourteen books[1] which are, so

---

1 Fourteen as reckoned in our English version. There are some variations in the count.

to speak, half in and half out of the Old Testament. The Old Testament properly so called is the corpus of books, written and handed down in Hebrew (or in the kindred Aramaic), which were received as Scripture in the first century of our era by Hebrew-speaking Jews, representing the central tradition of Hebrew and Jewish religion. The 'apocryphal' writings were handed down in Greek (though some of them were originally written in Hebrew), and they were accepted by Greek-speaking Jews, as part of their authoritative 'canon', along with the Hebrew Scriptures in a Greek translation. The attitude of the Church to what we may call the Greek-Jewish canon, as distinct from the Hebrew-Jewish, has varied at different periods and in different communions. What is important is the fact that the intention was to acknowledge as authoritative the sacred canon of the Jewish religion, whether this canon was defined more narrowly or more broadly. In fact, the Canon of Holy Scripture in the early Church, before the New Testament writings were collected, or even written, was simply the body of sacred writings taken over from Judaism. When New Testament writers refer to 'the Scriptures', they always (with two exceptions, in late-written books) mean what we call the Old Testament (with or without the Apocrypha). To this they refer with the greatest respect for its authority.

The Scriptures of the Jewish religion, then, are received by the Church as the sacred documents of the Old Covenant, setting forth God's relations with His people in the centuries before the coming of Jesus Christ. They record the inception of the covenant in the calling of Abraham, its establishment under Moses in the giving of the Law, and the vicissitudes, changes and developments in the relations of the covenanted people with their God, before the coming of Christ. Such is the main theme of the Old Testament, alike in narrative, poetry and prophecy.

In many of its writings we meet with a recurrent suggestion that the existing relations between God and His people under the covenant are in some measure incomplete or inconclusive. This sense of inconclusiveness grows, partly through the shock of a series of national calamities and their challenge to faith, and partly through deepening apprehension of what is implied in the idea of a covenant between God and man. It is put into words by one of the greatest of the prophets. Jeremiah spoke of a 'new covenant' which God would establish the other side of the disaster which he saw approaching.[1] The course of history gave to these words outstanding significance. The New Testament writers are unanimously of the belief that they have witnessed the establishment, by act of God, of the new covenant by which the relations between God and man escape all inconclusiveness and enter into their final phase. The new covenant does not simply supplement or modify the old; nor does it simply supersede it. It 'fulfils' it.

This idea of 'fulfilment' illuminates the paradox of newness and continuity to which I referred earlier. It carries two implications regarding our understanding of the biblical writings.

First, it is in the process of fulfilment that the Old Testament becomes intelligible. We of the present age are not the first to find difficulties in the Old Testament, for they are patent. The defective morals of some of its personages have caused much embarrassment. It contains incongruities and contradictions, not merely in matters of fact, but in spiritual outlook and moral valuation. The attempt to explain them away satisfies no alert and intelligent reader. We begin to understand them when we see them in their place in a process making towards an end. The road takes strange twists and turns, and leads through rough and uncertain places, but at any rate it reached the goal which is represented by the New Testament;

[1] Jeremiah xxxi. 31–34. See chap. iii, pp. 45–46.

and in view of that goal the incidents of the way disclose their meaning. The incongruities themselves illustrate the manner in which through trial and error men came to apprehend the truth; and the defects and limitations of which we are aware serve as background to the growing light which, as if evoked by them, shone upon the human scene.[1] Thus the Old Testament is not to be read as an odd collection of curious stories and ideas from a remote and primitive world, any more than it should be taken, on all its levels indiscriminately, as a definitive statement of unchanging truth. It is to be read in view of that for which it prepared and towards which it led. Of this more presently.

But, secondly, the New Testament, equally, is not to be understood apart from the Old. That needs to be said quite as emphatically as what I have just been saying. In the second century, at the time when the Canon of the New Testament was beginning to be formed, there was a controversy about the place which the Old Testament should occupy in the Church. There was a strong movement for abolishing it, just as there has been in more recent times; and largely on the same grounds—its defective morality and the inadequate or misleading conceptions of God which are to be found in it. A plausible case was made out for abandoning the Old Testament altogether and making the writings which we call the New Testament (or some of them) into a single and sufficient canon of Scripture. This proposal was emphatically rejected; and rightly so. It is its relation to this large and far-reaching background that gives depth to the New Testament presentation of religion. In modern times the tendency to study the New Testament in isolation from the Old has often distorted the perspective, and led to unnecessary difficulties about some of its leading ideas (such as, for example, the ideas of the Kingdom of God, of 'redemption' and 'justification') whose

1 For some illustrations of this see pp. 28–32.

true meaning stands out clearly when they are read in the light of all that went before.

It is, in a word, essential to our understanding of the Bible that we should hold its two parts together, as being mutually dependent.

The Bible, thus constituted of Old and New Testaments in unity, is the sacred book of the Christian religion; and we are now able to give a clearer sense to that definition than we were when it was enunciated at the beginning of this chapter. It is the book which the Church recommends people to read in order to know about God in His relation to man and the world, to worship Him intelligently, and to understand the aim and the obligations of human life under His rule. In other words, it offers this book to us as a 'revelation' of God. It refers us for this purpose to a long series of extremely various documents, containing many contradictions and incongruities, subject to the flow of time and change through many centuries of human existence.

This combination of 'things new and old' sets up a tension in the mind. But tension gives depth. And in fact, a tension of this kind is inseparable from our historical existence in a physical universe. The Bible reflects, with an astonishing realism, the existence of man as a creature living in the realm of time and space, and subject to change and development; and this makes it curiously relevant to human life, in its complexity, as we have to live it.

What do you take to be the terms of our own problem, whether as individuals or as a community, in this world, in the middle of the twentieth century? Is our problem simply that of yourself at twenty and myself at sixty, confronted with the world as presented in the pages of this morning's *Times*? If anyone thinks that no more than these factors are concerned in our problem, he is living in an illusion. Your problem and mine involves all the endeavours and achievements, failures and sins, that are covered by all the years we have lived. The living past survives into the present, as a deep stratum in our own minds. The child, they say, is father to the man, and any psychologist will tell you that the child within us may be a downright nuisance to the man, unless he has been put in his place.

Or consider the problems of the community. Think (to make the matter concrete) of the various conferences which are now beginning for the re-settlement of the world after the war. There will be certain persons visible at the conference table—representatives of contemporary nations in their corporate capacity. But there will be a much larger invisible concourse: kings and statesmen and adventurers of the past, Holy Roman Emperors and mediaeval Popes, vikings and tribal chiefs, Czars, mandarins and shoguns, and all the dumb multitudes of the dead, whose actions, deliberate or undesigned, went to make up the world of nations as it is to-day. These unseen presences will press their claims through the enduring facts of history, which we cannot alter for our convenience.

The complexity of our problem, in short, arises from our situation in an historical process subject to time and change, irreversible in direction, in which the past is never wholly dead, but remains unalterably part of the situation we have to face in the present.

It is here that the Bible is so singularly appropriate to the conditions of our problem, individual and corporate. It is offered to us by the Church as a revelation of God; not, certainly, as a sort of inspired encyclopaedia, where chapter and verse can be turned up and questions settled out of hand. On the contrary, it first makes us aware of the depth and range of our problem, rooted as it is in the remote but still living past. It plunges us into the stream of history in a peculiarly significant part of its course. It makes present to us crucial events of the past by which the stream cut for itself the channel in which it still sweeps us along—such events as the call of Abraham, the Exodus and the giving of the Law, the Exile and return of the Jews, and that climax of the whole drama recorded in the Gospels, which, as we shall presently see, controls and interprets it all.[1] It is history, of the same stuff as our contemporary history; of the same stuff as our individual experience of day-to-day happenings. But it is so presented that it is seen to be full of meaning, as our lives are not, as contemporary history is not, so far as we can see. The biblical history is meaningful because it is related at every point to the fundamental reality which lies behind all history and all human experience, which is, the living God in His Kingdom; and because it moves towards a climax in which the Kingdom of God came upon men with conclusive effect.

In this presentation of the movement of history the oddities and incongruities of the record have their indispensable place, because they correspond to the real complexities of human experience in this world. It all reaches unity through fulfilment, and in the light of this fulfilment we are invited to recognize the hand of God in the whole process.

The way in which we are to pass from the recognition of God in the biblical history to the recognition of Him as speaking through it to *us*, is a subject which must occupy us later.[2] For the present, we may answer the question propounded at the beginning by saying that the Bible is a unity of diverse writings which together are set forth by the Church as a revelation of God in history.

1 See chap. IV, pp. 93–96; chap. V, pp. 106–111.
2 See chap. VII.

CHAPTER II

THE APPROACH TO THE BIBLE

THE CHURCH, we have seen, offers the Bible, in both testaments, as the authoritative record of a divine revelation in history. The Old Testament was accepted as such from the very first. Indeed, one can hardly speak of the Church as 'accepting' the Old Testament. The Old Testament was there, and the Church grew up in dependence upon it. Gradually the writings of the New Testament came to be placed upon an equal footing of authority, and in the end the whole corpus of writings was acknowledged as 'Holy Scripture'.

This recognition did not in early times carry with it any objection to free and candid criticism of the writings of the Old and New Testaments. It seems necessary to say this because it is often supposed that biblical criticism is an invention of the 'Age of Reason', to be hailed as an example of our superior enlightenment or reprobated as an act of irreverence according to taste. But this is a mistake. The foundations of biblical criticism were laid in the first four centuries of the Christian era. A most comprehensive and thorough critical edition of the text of the Old Testament was produced in the third century by that very great Christian scholar, Origen of Caesarea. There was a considerable amount of critical discussion upon such questions as the authorship of various writings, and their relative value, upon contradictions in the Old Testament and divergences among the four Gospels. Such discussion was informed by the excellent principles and methods of Greek scholarship. To take one instance, there is preserved an admirable piece of biblical criticism from the middle of the third century by Bishop

Dionysius of Alexandria. He reviews the evidence for the authorship of the book of Revelation. He challenges the generally accepted view that it was written by the Apostle John. He argues from a comparison with the Fourth Gospel that the two writings could not have come from the same pen. His arguments have never been effectively answered and, although his view did not prevail in antiquity, modern critical scholarship almost unanimously supports his conclusion.

More important still is the freedom of interpretation which we find in these early biblical students. Such freedom was indispensable when the Jewish canon was taken over by the Church. From the beginning it was assumed that the Old Testament was in part abrogated by the Gospel. Just how far abrogation went was matter for discussion. Since some people wanted to throw the Old Testament overboard, the question needed careful treatment. It could be approached only through a scholarly consideration and comparison of a great variety of texts, and a sustained attempt to ascertain their true meaning.

It was assumed that the Old Testament as a whole needed interpreting in the light of the new teachings of Christianity. To the task of re-interpretation the leaders of Christian thought gave diligent attention. In dealing with the problem, they made free use of an allegorical method of interpretation, which was a legacy from ancient Greek scholarship. A familiar example of this method is to be found in the chapter-headings provided in older editions of our Authorised Version for the Song of Solomon. The book appears to be a sequence of love-lyrics. The chapter-headings, following a long tradition, interpret them with reference to the mystical loves of Christ and the Church. That is rather an extreme example.

The allegorical method however, within its proper limits, is by no means without justification or legitimate use. There are unquestionably parts of the Bible where the real meaning intended by the author is not the plain literal sense of the words, and where an unintelligent insistence upon the literal sense stands in the way of a true understanding.

There is a clear case in the Book of Jonah. The famous 'whale', or rather sea-monster[1], is no zoological specimen. The ancient monster of chaos, the dragon of darkness, was a familiar figure in several mythologies of the ancient world, and the story how a god or hero was swallowed by the monster but made his victorious escape, was widely known, and carried a well-recognized symbolic meaning. When the Gospel according to Matthew uses the story of Jonah as a symbol of resurrection from the dead,[2] it is not very far from the original intention of the myth. It seems probable that the author of the Book of Jonah applied it to the resurrection of the Israelite nation after its submergence by the Babylonian conquest.[3] In any case, we are dealing here with symbolism, and a recognition of this fact might have saved much embarrassment.

This is not the only case of the kind. The element of symbolism is deeply embedded in the structure of biblical thought. It pervades the poetical language of the prophets, and enters into the parables of the Gospels. Again, religious ritual is inherently symbolical wherever it occurs, and not least in the Bible. The prophets, too, were accustomed to perform actions having about them something of the solemnity of ritual, with the intention that they should symbolize truths which they wished to enunciate.[4] It would clearly be a mistake to

1 Jonah i. 17.   2 Matthew xii. 40.

3 Cf. p. 48.

4 E.g. Jeremiah xix. 1–2, 10–13 (the prophet smashes an earthenware jar to symbolize the completeness of the destruction awaiting Jerusalem), xxvii. 2 (he wears a yoke to symbolize the 'subjugation' of the peoples); Ezekiel iv. 1–3 (the prophet makes a model of a besieged city with a tile and an iron pan to symbolize the siege of Jerusalem). In such cases the symbolism is on the surface. A similar symbolic intention may well provide the key to some rather puzzling stories.

tie down such writers to the bare literal sense of their words in every case.

There is a further point. Any great event which stirs the imagination gathers about it an 'aura' of emotional significance which translates it into a symbol, and the symbol may grow in meaning with the process of time. Most nations have such symbolic events in their tradition. Think, for example, of the place held in our own tradition by such an event as the signing of Magna Carta, or the defeat of the Spanish Armada. In like manner the emancipation, or 'redemption', of Israel from Egyptian servitude by the crossing of the Red Sea came to stand as a symbol, first, of God's providence over His people, and then of the 'redemption' of mankind in a far deeper sense.[1]

There is therefore a sound basis for the use of the allegorical method in interpreting the Scriptures. Although it too easily gets out of hand, yet the contrary error of a bald and prosaic literalism may easily miss the full meaning. In the biblical exegesis of the early Church the method had a real value. It gave freedom from the tyranny of already antiquated forms of thought; freedom from the necessity of accepting at their face value, as part of a divine revelation, puerile and sometimes revolting survivals from primitive times. It gave an opening, of which some of the finest minds took full advantage, for a genuinely imaginative treatment of the Bible; and the role of imagination in the apprehension of religious truth should never be under-estimated, though imagination should not be allowed to decline into fantasy.

But while all this is true, it is also true that the over-free use of allegory has a flattening and blunting effect. It is fatally easy to escape the full impact of a difficult passage by giving it a non-natural meaning. Anything can stand for anything else, and nothing has any sharp outline.

1 See, e.g., Deuteronomy vii. 8; Psalm cxxx. 8; I Peter i. 18.

It is a good rule that in trying to understand the Bible one should not have recourse to a figurative or allegorical explanation of any passage (outside those poetical and prophetical compositions which obviously have a symbolic intention) without first settling conclusions with the straightforward meaning, even if it seems offensive; for the offence may set up that tension in the mind through which we often reach the truth.[1]

It seemed worth while saying this, because in these last years there has been a renewed interest in these half-forgotten methods of biblical interpretation. It is to be welcomed so far as it frees the study of the Bible, and especially of the Old Testament, from an arid historical literalism; but it has grave dangers, dangers which were certainly not altogether avoided by the allegorists of the early and mediaeval Church, and of which their modern followers should be aware.

However that may be, the sustained labours of generations of early biblical scholars gradually established certain broad controlling principles of interpretation; and these ultimately crystallized into a general *schema*, by which the study of the Bible was henceforth to be directed. It rested upon a true, if in some respects limited, understanding of the two testaments in their historical relations. At any rate it emerged out of the Bible itself, and was not imposed upon it.

In this *schema*, the Old Testament appears as a series of prophecies and 'types' which are 'fulfilled' in the New Testament. Not only the words of the prophets, but also the actions that make up Old Testament history, foreshadow the action as well as the thought of the New Testament. This twofold structure of history—prophecy and fulfilment, type and antitype—is rounded off at the beginning by the story of the Creation and Fall of man, and at the end by the Last Judgement; but the central and decisive place is held by that which is central in the New Testament: the proclamation of the coming

1 For an example, see pp. 28–29.

of Christ—His birth, life, death and resurrection—as the controlling fact of all history, whether before or after, from which the meaning of it all is to be understood.

This *schema* provided a framework for Christian thought and devotion all through the Middle Ages. It shaped the pattern of the Church's services for the Christian Year, with their lessons from the Old and New Testaments, and their liturgical Gospels and Epistles. It is illustrated in the religious art of the period, notably in the stained glass which once adorned the windows of our parish churches. Where the original arrangement of glass can still be seen complete (as, for example, at Fairford in the Cotswolds), you walk up the nave with prophets on your left, uttering their predictions of things to come, and apostles and evangelists on your right, announcing the fulfilment. You thus approach the east end of the church, where the whole Gospel drama is illustrated scene by scene, from the Annunciation of the birth of Christ to His Ascension. Then you turn about, to be confronted by the great west window, with its flaming picture of Doomsday.

How far the Bible was familiar to the laity—or to the ordinary parish priest, for that matter—during the Middle Ages, is a question upon which mediaeval historians appear to differ; but it is safe to say that what knowledge of the Bible there was lay within the *schema*, which gave the key to its understanding. Broadly speaking, it is probably true to say that the Church was more concerned to communicate the *schema* to the laity than the Bible itself; but in doing so it ensured that whatever of the biblical material became available, either by direct reading, or through liturgy and offices, through sermons, hymns or pictures, was seen in a well-defined perspective.

During the fourteenth and fifteenth centuries a movement set in for popularizing the Scriptures. In this country, it produced the first complete English translation of the Bible, which was directly inspired by the teaching of John Wycliffe. His contention was that the laity, being God's vassals, should be able to instruct themselves in His law (every private in the army of the Lord, so to speak, should have access to King's Regulations). This movement paved the way for the Reformation of the sixteenth century. The restoration of the Bible to the laity was a major plank in the reformers' platform. If, as the Church had always taught, the Bible contained God's revelation to man, every man (they urged) ought to be able to read it for himself, and not to be dependent upon what might reach him by indirect channels.

In thus opening the entire Canon of Scripture to the free study of the laity, the reformers did not intend to abandon the ancient framework within which it was to be understood. They themselves were well-instructed in the traditional *schema*, and it controlled the biblical theology of Calvin, for example, not less than that of mediaeval theologians. But in placing the Bible at the disposal of the uninstructed they took a fateful step. It could now be read, and was widely read, 'without note or comment', without the guidance which had been supplied by tradition. To allow and encourage this was inevitably to admit the right of private judgement in interpreting it. In the course of controversy the reformers were led to go further than they had intended at first, and to claim for the whole Bible indiscriminately, in and by itself, exposed as it now was to the possible vagaries of private interpretation, an absolute authority displacing that of the Catholic Church. The Church of Rome replied by an increased rigidity in its control of Bible-reading. The cleavage which ensued had unfortunate results.

In the Churches of the Reformation the immediate result was, undeniably, an outburst of religious spontaneity such as marks periods of expansion and revival, comparable with prophetic movements in the early Church and in the history of the Old Testament. The enthusiasm with which the Bible was read, and its sublime utterances greeted, by those to whom they came for the first time in their own tongue, as something entirely fresh, set free spiritual energy in creative ways. Parts of the Bible which under the rigidity of the traditional *schema* had lost vital interest now seemed to disclose unsuspected wealth of meaning to awakened and liberated minds.

But there was another side to it. The claim that the Bible could be read, just as it stood, without the guidance of tradition, and with equal authority attaching to all its parts, exposed it to the dangers of a chaotic individualism. Where there was no longer any common standard or perspective, the line was not easily drawn between a just freedom of responsible judgement and the play of arbitrary preference. It was this state of affairs that evoked the satirical epigram,

> Hic liber est in quo quaerit sua dogmata quisque;
> Invenit et pariter dogmata quisque sua.

(This is the book where everyone seeks his own proper opinion;
This is the book where still everyone finds what he seeks.)

It is impossible to question the immense stimulus, spiritual and intellectual, which a large part of Christendom received from the opening up of the Bible at the Reformation. But it is equally impossible to deny that the reformed communions and sects were exposed to the risk of its less favourable results. On the one hand the maxim, 'The Bible and the Bible alone is the religion of Protestants', was construed in a way which demanded that equal and absolute authority should be accorded to every part of the Old and New Testaments indiscriminately, since it was all 'verbally inspired'. No doubt sensible people always found ways of evading the more obviously absurd consequences of such a view; but it went far to hinder a just understanding of the Bible in its integrity. On the other hand, the demand for unqualified freedom of interpretation opened the way to limitless aberrations. An extreme example is to be found in the exploitation of the more obscure 'apocalyptic' writings[1] such as the Book of Daniel in the Old Testament and the book of Revelation in the New, which became the licensed playground of every crank. Short of such extremes, however, an irresponsible use of freedom, especially in the interests of controversy, often led to loss of a just perspective and distorted the proportions of the biblical picture.

Then came the revival of biblical criticism, and the modern period began. Some years ago, before the Four Years' War, a daily paper initiated a 'silly season' correspondence on the subject, 'Should parsons criticize the Bible?' To this *Punch* replied by posing the question, 'Should railway porters criticize Bradshaw?' Apparently Mr Punch's young men associated the term 'criticism' with the idea of censure or fault-finding, which the word does often imply, as used colloquially. It is probable that some prejudice against biblical criticism has been aroused among religious persons by this half-conscious association of ideas. But it is hardly necessary to say that a biblical 'critic' is not one who sets himself above the Bible and points out its defects. Biblical criticism means nothing but applying to the biblical documents the rational or scientific methods of scholarship which are applied in other fields of study.

As we have seen, the great theologians of the early Church practised biblical criticism. Much of the information that has come down to us by tradition about the authorship, place and date of biblical writings, about differences of text and translation, and the like, is the outcome of intelligent critical discussion which took place between the first century and the fourth. After that the discussion was virtually closed down for some centuries. The problems were assumed to be solved, and authority guaranteed the solutions.

Critical scholarship came back to Western Europe with the

1 On apocalyptic writings see pp. 60–64.

revival of classical studies at the Renaissance. The new learning penetrated slowly into our field. It was during the eighteenth and nineteenth centuries that biblical criticism made its most serious advances.

It is usual to speak of 'higher' and 'lower' criticism. The terms are singularly infelicitous, but they have established themselves in usage. 'Lower criticism' attempts to restore the original text of a book, when it has been subject to variation in the course of transmission. With books which, like those of the Bible, were transmitted in manuscript for many centuries, the possibilities of variation are very great, and the work of textual criticism (as it is better called) is correspondingly serious. 'Higher criticism' discusses such questions as those of date, authorship, relation to other documents; it compares documents with one another, notes divergences or contradictions, and attempts to determine between them. It is with 'higher' criticism that we are here mainly concerned.

It is characteristic of modern biblical criticism that it employs the historical method. This means that questions of chronology bulk largely. This may seem a dull business. What indeed could be duller than 'dates'? But to get the documents into the right order is the first step towards studying them intelligently as records of an historical process; and as we have seen, that is what the Bible is. In fact it is not too much to say that biblical criticism met the post-Reformation confusion, in which the unity once imposed by the traditional *schema* had been largely lost, by imposing upon the Bible a new unity, that of an ascertained chronological succession of events and of movements of thought.

I may illustrate this point from a neighbouring field of study. I have been reading a little book recently published under the title *The Three Ages*, by Dr Glyn Daniel. It describes the beginning of the scientific study of pre-historic man. In 1816 a Danish antiquarian named Thomsen was appointed curator of the newly formed National Museum at Copenhagen. His first task was to arrange his collection of antiquities. To bring some order into the mass of pre-historic remains which lay about in confusion, he sorted them out on the basis of the materials used for weapons and implements—stone, bronze and iron. It then occurred to him that this was not a mere classification for convenience, but represented a chronological sequence —Stone Age, Bronze Age, Iron Age. Subsequent excavation proved that the three ages were historical facts, and the foundation was laid upon which our modern knowledge of early man has been built. The historical critics perform a somewhat similar service to biblical study.

Anyone can see that the Old and New Testaments contain a mass of disparate material, often perplexing in its variety. Criticism not only sorts it out, but arranges it in a chronological order and establishes relations between the various parts. It does this, not by guess work, and certainly not by indulging personal preference or caprice, but by employing scientific methods of observation, analysis, hypothesis and verification, which are well tested in other fields of study. It is a rational and scientific discipline, and its findings are true or untrue according to the evidence in each particular case. If such findings are often tentative or uncertain, it is because of the nature of the subject-matter, and such uncertainty does not discredit the method. The results may be challenged on this point or that: it is a matter of evidence and of the competence of the person who is dealing with it. As a special branch of study it aims at being objective, rational, scientific. Its methods may in future be improved, its presuppositions revised, but it stands firm as a self-justifying part of the reasonable search for knowledge, and its abandonment would be a 'flight from reason'.

The nineteenth-century critics, however, worked, like all of us, under the influence of the intellectual climate of their time. It was the time when the newly enunciated theory of evolution was becoming dominant over the whole field of the natural sciences, and seemed to many minds to have provided, at last, a universal key to knowledge of the world and of man. Like other historians, the historical critics of the Bible made it their aim to interpret the course of human history on the analogy of biological evolution. The reconstruction of the biblical history which they produced is now commonly called the 'liberal' view—though the term 'liberal' is here used in a sense originally German rather than English, and should not be made a stick to beat those who are 'liberal' in a different sense. It is not the result of a purely objective analysis of the documents. It presupposes a particular theory about the nature of history, and the evidence of the documents is interpreted in subordination to that theory. Looking back, we can see that this presupposition has often given a distorting bias to the work of the critics. In other fields of historical investigation (and notably in pre-history) it now appears that the earlier evolutionary reconstructions were over-simplified [1]; and so is the 'liberal', evolutionary reconstruction of the biblical history.

What is more important, the earlier critics did less than justice to the fact that the Bible has its own doctrine about the nature of history, which deserves to be understood and appreciated in itself. What the biblical view of history is, we shall have to enquire later.[2] For the present we note that the association of biblical criticism with the 'liberal' interpretation of biblical history is accidental, and needs to be re-examined.

We have in fact moved during recent years into a new period of biblical study, which may be described as 'post-liberal': not however 'post-critical'. The critical method is not antiquated, even though some of the earlier critical views must

1 Cf., e.g., Glyn Daniel, *op. cit.* pp. 16, 23–24, etc.
2 See chap. v.

be revised. If we are bound to criticize the great critics of the last century, we are also bound to confess that where we have gone beyond them it is by standing on their shoulders. It is a testimony to the scientific integrity of the critical school that by applying its own methods more strictly it was led to discard many of the presuppositions upon which it formerly relied, and to arrive at what I believe to be a juster estimate of the material with which it deals. Be suspicious of any suggestion that we can afford to by-pass criticism. The way of advance lies through and not round the critical problem.

Granted, however, that biblical criticism is a legitimate, and even a useful, branch of scientific study, is it important for the general reader, who has no particular interest in matters of archaeology or ancient history? It is quite true that it has accumulated, like any other special science, a vast and complex mass of detail which does not greatly matter to anyone but the specialist. I should be sorry to suggest that the only way to an understanding of the Bible lies through the latest refinements of critical scholarship. But the problems with which criticism is concerned are problems that face any reader who wishes to understand the Scriptures, and the critical *method*, as a means of approach to the Scriptures, is acutely relevant to any serious study of the Bible as a religious book.

To begin with, since the Bible comes to us (as we have seen) as a revelation of divine truth in the form of a history of events, the principle of succession in time is essential to it. Revelation is not what the cinema trade (I believe) calls a 'still'; it is a moving picture. It is a drama. Or if you will, it is a musical symphony. The film, the drama, the symphony, conveys its meaning and value by movement. The movement is essential to it, even though in the end movement is transcended in a unity of apprehension. So with the Bible. The movement of events is the instrument through which truth is conveyed—the movement of events, and the movement of thought; for the movement of thought also is history, and the writing of the Book of Job or the Epistle to the Romans is an event, and part of the succession of events through which the unity of revelation is given. Consequently the correct placing of documents in an historical series is a part of the study of revelation.

It is only by grasping this fact that we arrive at a satisfying answer to the problem presented by the crudities and imperfections of certain parts of the Bible. These crudities and imperfections play their part in the process of revelation, in the act of being transcended by something higher. Let us take an example.

Any humane mind is revolted by the accounts of atrocities recorded to have been committed by the Israelites during the conquest of Palestine, and recorded without any expression of disapproval. 'Go and smite Amalek...and spare them not; but slay both man and woman, infant and suckling, ox and sheep, camel and ass.'[1] When such injunctions have been taken at their face value, they have had disastrous effects upon the moral judgements, and the actions, of Christian people; as when Cromwell's devout troopers massacred the 'idolatrous' Irish Catholics of Drogheda (just as centuries earlier, the pious Simon de Montfort exterminated the Albigensian heretics). In the main tradition of Christian teaching the Amalekites are taken to be a symbol for the 'spiritual hosts of wickedness' with which we are to contend *à outrance*. Upon this assumption the whole story becomes not only innocuous, but edifying. But the prophet who gave that bloodthirsty command, and the writer who recorded it, were not thinking of spiritual adversaries. They honestly thought

[1] Read the story in I Samuel xv. It is the more pointed because obedience to this revolting command is taken as a test of loyalty to God, and Saul's faint leaning to mercy is unsparingly condemned.

that the ruthless extermination of that unfortunate border tribe was well-pleasing to God. We may say that such ruthlessness was, at that primitive stage, inseparable from the stern discipline by which the clans of Israel were separated from their neighbours and made ready to bear witness to an exclusive loyalty to one God, unique in the ancient world. But before that witness could become effective the whole idea of a divinely sanctioned brutality had to be purged from the system. The distance travelled between Samuel's 'Go and utterly destroy those sinners the Amalekites!' and the Gospel precept, 'Love your enemies',[1] is the measure of the way we have to travel, following the movement of the biblical history,[2] in discerning the will of God. The Gospel precept challenges, not simply our unreasoning and unworthy hatreds, but those hatreds which we feel, as did the early Israelites, we *ought* to cherish ('Do I not hate them, O Lord, that hate Thee? ....I hate them with perfect hatred'[3]). If at this moment the shoe pinches hard, then we are experiencing the tension through which truth becomes our own possession.

Thus we may face the scandal and offence which some parts of the Bible offer to the mind, without timidly attempting to explain them away. Indeed, whether or not they present this kind of difficulty, we can afford to give full weight to

1 Matthew v. 44.

2 We may note one particular milestone on the way. About 840 B.C. Jehu, incited by the prophet Elisha, rebelled against King Joram. The rebellion was successful. Jehu treacherously massacred the entire royal family at their residence of Jezreel, as well as vast numbers of their adherents, whom the prophet regarded as idolators. Jehu was confident that he was winning merit. 'Come with me, and see my zeal for the Lord', he called out as he drove to the scene of the massacre (II Kings ix–x). A century later another prophet, Hosea (i. 4), bitterly condemns the 'blood-bath of Jezreel'. The change of attitude is associated with a new conception of the character of God. See pp. 41–42.

3 Psalm cxxxix. 21–22.

the plain, original meaning of the documents. The writer may speak for himself, and say to us exactly what he meant to say to his first readers. We require no crude attempts to 'modernize' his words. We listen to him with the humility which will not interrupt him in order to square what he says with what we think he ought to have said. We shall allow him to give his own answers to his own questions, and not insist that he must always be answering ours. The true meaning of any positive statement depends on the question to which it is the answer. One service that the historical approach to the Bible can render is to make us aware of the questions that lay before the writers, so that we understand their answers before we apply them to our own problems.

For example, the first chapter in the Bible, which gives an account of the creation of the world, caused much searching of heart to an earlier generation of readers, just because the question was wrongly put. At that time people were much exercised by the new researches into the origin of species and kindred problems. They assumed that the first chapter of Genesis gave the biblical answer to the same questions as those which occupied modern biologists and geologists, an answer not acceptable to the scientific mind. But in fact the author of that chapter was not concerned with the scientific problem of the origin of species. Critical analysis helps to put the matter in the right perspective.

It shows that the first chapter of Genesis is a relatively late composition. We have in the second chapter an earlier, and cruder, Hebrew story of creation. The account in the first chapter was written after the prophets had done their great work towards a purer and more spiritual religion. At that time there were many stories of creation current among the Israelites and their neighbours, relics of a ruder age. The Babylonians, for example, among whom the Jews lived in exile, told (with much picturesque detail) how the

Creator-god had fought and overcome the monster of chaos, cut her in halves, and made heaven of one half and earth of the other. There is reason to believe that a rather similar story once had a vogue among the Israelites themselves. How could a Creator so conceived be offered the spiritual worship which the prophets had taught? For that matter, what are we to say about the story in the second chapter of Genesis— how God made a clay model of a man and brought it to life by breathing on it? We may read it, in the light of a long-established allegorical tradition, as a parable of deeper truths; but to the Jews of the fifth century B.C., who took it at its face value, the Hebrew story, though not grotesque like the Babylonian, was too ingenuous and childlike to command the 'reverence and godly fear' which belongs to all high religion. This, then, was the question which faced religious teachers of the time: How may we speak of the mystery of the Creator's relation to His world, so as to do justice to the majesty and transcendence of the one God, and to evoke the reverent worship which is His due?

Now read what one of them has written:

In the beginning God created the heaven and the earth.
> And the earth was waste and void;
> And darkness was upon the face of the deep;
> And the spirit of God moved upon the face of the waters.
And God said, 'Let there be light!'
> And there was light.

So the story proceeds, in a vein of pure imagination, stripped of all puerile fancies, to evoke the idea of a God who 'spake and it was done'. His *word*, the utterance of a thinking Mind and a deliberate Will, illuminates the dark abyss of nothingness, and calls into being things that are not.

This is the intention of the creation-story of Genesis i. The question before its author lay not in the field of scientific matter of fact, but in the field of religious truth. His answer will give us no help towards solving the problems of physics and biology, but if we ask the deeper and more fundamental questions about the nature of God and His relation to man and the world, then his answer has permanent relevance. His idea of the creative Word, in fact, holds a commanding position in the history of thought,[1] and, in its developed form, it has become central to the philosophy of the Christian religion.

This will serve to illustrate the point that a critical and historical approach to the biblical writings puts us in the way of understanding their meaning more precisely, because we allow the writers to speak for themselves, giving their own answers to their own questions. These questions will not always be those that are occupying our minds at the moment. Very often the best service that our reading can do us is to raise prior questions, questions which need to be asked and answered before we can profitably consider the immediate problems, private or public, practical or theoretical, upon which we should wish to get light. Nothing is more certain than that an intelligent reading of the Bible does bring effective guidance in the most urgent and actual present problems; but to get it we must submit ourselves to the discipline of listening to words that were not intended for us at all.

We have seen that at one period a rigid scheme of interpretation tended to blanket the direct impact of the Bible upon the mind; and at another period the license of private interpretation threatened to befog it in a cloud of individual predilections. The critical method finds its way between the horns of the dilemma. It rejects restraint from without upon liberty of interpretation, and at the same time excludes an arbitrary or capricious use of liberty by accepting the intrinsic control of the historical movement within the Bible itself.

In what follows our approach to the Bible will be critical and historical.

1 See also chap. v, pp. 107–109.

CHAPTER III

THE OLD TESTAMENT

I T will be useful to start with a rough outline of the chronology of the writings of the Old Testament, based upon generally accepted conclusions of biblical criticism.

Century B.C.

XIII (or earlier?) Exodus from Egypt ⎫
XII (?) Settlement in Palestine ⎪ Oral traditions (laws,
XI Wars with Canaanites, etc. ⎬ legends, poems) pre-
Foundation of Monarchy ⎪ served in later writ-
(David, 1000 B.C.). ⎭ ings.

X Court chronicles begin (incorporated in later books).

IX Early laws and traditions written down: Judaean collection ('J') and Ephraimite collection ('E'), later incorporated in Genesis-to-Joshua.

VIII Amos, Hosea, Micah, Isaiah. (Fall of Samaria, 721.)

VII Josiah's Reformation, 621. Deuteronomy, Jeremiah, Zephaniah, Nahum.

VI Habakkuk, Judges, Samuel, Kings. (Fall of Jerusalem, 586.) Ezekiel, 'II Isaiah', Haggai, Zechariah.

V 'Priestly' laws and narratives of Genesis-to-Joshua ('P') written on basis of earlier traditions. Malachi, Job.

IV Compilation of Genesis-to-Joshua (out of 'J', 'E', 'P' and Deuteronomy.)

III Chronicles, Ecclesiastes.

II Book of Psalms completed (largely out of much earlier poems). Ecclesiasticus, Daniel, etc.

I Book of Wisdom, etc.

You will observe that not one of the books of the Old Testament (in its finished form) is of earlier date than the eighth century B.C. Before that time there existed traditions handed down by word of mouth, and various documentary records and compositions, which were used by later writers. But the books of the Old Testament, as we know them, were composed in the period starting with the great prophets Amos, Hosea, Micah and Isaiah. And it was the work of these prophets which directly or indirectly determined the character of the Canon of Scripture. Their stamp is in one way or another upon it all.

Much of the pre-prophetic material comes down from very early ages indeed. Its value lies largely in enabling us to see how the whole history of revelation with which the Bible is concerned is rooted in the good red earth of our common humanity; in primitive, elemental human affections and passions, the groundwork still of all our life, however sophisticated and civilized we have become. That is why the old 'Bible stories' which have been told to children for so many centuries keep their appeal. But the books in which they have come down to us are deeply marked with the influence of the prophets. It is through the key provided by prophetic teaching that they yield their meaning for religion.

We shall start therefore with the great prophets who wrote during the two centuries from 750 to 550 B.C. (roughly).

First, let us review the course of events in these two centuries.

The curtain rises upon two small kingdoms of kindred blood and speech, occupying the territory now known as Palestine: the Kingdom of Judah in the south, with its capital at Jerusalem, and the Kingdom of Israel (or of Ephraim) in the north, with its capital at Samaria. We might think of Holland and Belgium, or, more appropriately, of Latvia and Esthonia, because the two little Palestinian kingdoms, like those ill-fated republics, were 'buffer-states' between two great powers, Egypt and Assyria. The rivalry of these two powers provides the background for the whole drama of the history of the Israelite kingdoms.

In the middle of the eighth century B.C. there was a period of comparative peace; and the northern kingdom, under its king, Jeroboam II, was enjoying the unwonted luxuries of military superiority over its immediate neighbours and of commercial prosperity. The country was becoming relatively wealthy and civilized. But the growth of wealth and refinement had the kind of effect it often has. It was already leading to divisions within the nation, which ultimately proved fatal to it. Meanwhile the storm-clouds of Assyrian aggression were gathering on the horizon. Before long they broke. When the government awoke to the situation, there were the usual efforts at 'appeasement', hasty feeling about for possible alliances, and then a belated and desperate resistance, which was finally broken. The country was overrun by the enemy, its capital city destroyed, a large part of its population deported, and the vacant territory appropriated by foreign settlers. That was the end of the Kingdom of Israel.

The tide of invasion swept southwards to the Kingdom of Judah. Under the conquering king Sennacherib it looked as if history would repeat itself, and Jerusalem and Judah would go the way of the northern kingdom. Sennacherib has left his own account of the campaign. 'Hezekiah the Jew,' he writes, 'I shut up like a bird in a cage.' From within the beleaguered city we have Isaiah's war-commentary.[1]

> Your country is desolate;
> Your cities are burned with fire;
> Your land, strangers devour it in your presence,
> And it is desolate, as overthrown by strangers.
> And the daughter of Zion is left,
> As a booth in a vineyard,
> As a lodge in a garden of cucumbers,
> As a besieged city.

[1] Isaiah i. 7–9.

3-2

Except the Lord of hosts had left us a very small
remnant,
We should have been as Sodom;
We should have been like unto Gomorrah.

The city was summoned to surrender. King Hezekiah refused.
There is a vivid description of the negotiations in the Second
Book of Kings, and in the Book of Isaiah.[1] (It provides an
early example of what we should call 'psychological warfare'!) Nothing, it seemed, could save the doomed city. Then
the unexpected happened. The Assyrian commander with-
drew his forces and retired. It is one of the unexplained
decisive happenings in the history of warfare, like Von
Kluck's blunder at the Marne in 1914, and perhaps Hitler's
failure to invade Britain in 1940. Why the Assyrians retired,
we cannot say. The Greek historian Herodotus was told
that the Assyrian archers had their bowstrings gnawed by
mice. The Book of Kings uses language which might suggest
an epidemic.[2] (Were Herodotus's 'mice' really rats carrying
bubonic plague?) Since Sennacherib's position was shortly
afterwards shaken both by foreign attack and by internal revolt,
in which he ultimately perished, it is possible that news of
disturbances at home recalled him.[3] We do not know. At
any rate Judah obtained a respite.

After a troubled interval the intelligent and forceful king
Josiah succeeded in establishing his authority, and even ex-
tended it over part of the lost territories in the north. Adopting
a policy of centralization, he carried through an ambitious
programme of civil and religious reforms. But there was no
possibility of real independence for the small nations, as
Palestine became once more the cockpit of rival empires, and
Josiah died leaving his kingdom a dependency of the Egyptian
crown.

1 II Kings xviii. 13–37; Isaiah xxxvi.
2 II Kings xix. 35–36.   3 Cf. II Kings xix. 7, 37.

The power of Assyria collapsed; but the collapse meant little more than a change of dynasty, for Babylon seized the sceptre, and under its king Nebuchadnezzar quickly restored the situation. Nebuchadnezzar may be said to have had a 'bad press' in the Old Testament, but he was an able and enlightened monarch—statesman, soldier and builder. He set about recovering the territories Assyria had lost. Sooner or later Judah would lie in his path. The sons and grand-sons of Josiah were a pitiable lot. They swithered between Egypt and Babylon, playing each side false in turn. Mis-governed and divided by faction, the kingdom was a ready prey to the Babylonian conqueror. The end came when the wretched king Zedekiah abandoned his beleaguered and famine-stricken capital, and fled with his army by night, only to be captured by the enemy. Jerusalem was sacked, its temple demolished, its fortifications dismantled, and a large part of the population deported, including the nobility and gentry and the skilled craftsmen. All that remained was an ignorant and impoverished peasantry, trying to bring back a 'scorched' earth into cultivation. That was the end of the Kingdom of Judah.[1]

The exiles in Babylon were not ill-treated. The Babylonians were a highly civilized mercantile people. Clever and in-dustrious settlers like the Jews easily made a place for them-selves in the life of their adopted country. There seemed no reason why they should not be comfortably assimilated into the general body of the Babylonian Empire, like many con-quered peoples before them. But almost from the moment of the collapse a group of patriotic and far-sighted men began to work on plans for the reconstruction of the Jewish state.

[1] The miserable story is told briefly in II Kings xxiii. 31–xxv. 22, but the internal situation is most vividly portrayed in the rich col-lection of contemporary poems, orations, and biographical anecdotes which we have in the Book of Jeremiah.

They had no obvious grounds for thinking that their plans would come to anything, but they believed they would, and persevered.

Half a century later Babylon fell, and Cyrus the Persian took over the reins of empire. He gave permission for Jewish exiles to return to Jerusalem, if they wished to do so. A small handful did return, followed later by others. They re-founded the Jewish community among the ruins of Jerusalem, and by slow and painful degrees built up a civil and ecclesiastical polity through which the Jewish people maintained and developed its national traditions under the tolerant rule of the Persian Empire.[1]

Such, in broad outlines, was the course of events during these fateful two centuries. It is well established by ample documentary evidence, from Hebrew and from foreign sources. Perhaps it does not appear very remarkable. Other small nations have declined and fallen, and have risen again. Why should we attach to this piece of history an uncommon importance? To answer that question we must go through the period again, looking at events from the inside, with the help of the contemporary writings of the prophets, which form a kind of continuous commentary upon history. The events in themselves are just things that happened, plain matter of fact, like the events announced in the B.B.C. news this morning. But the prophets represent history as something more than a mere succession of events; as something that has *meaning*; and that meaning is of the highest importance.

First, then, Amos, a sheep-farmer from the comparatively poor and backward south, came into the northern kingdom at the height of its short period of hectic prosperity in the reign of Jeroboam II. He observed the effects of growing wealth and luxury, and recognized behind the façade of economic prosperity the symptoms of social decline. Society

1 On the character of the restored community, see p. 3.

(38)

was rotten with sensuality, injustice and the oppression of the poor, and this was, in his eyes, an affront to God. The national religion, it is true, enjoyed a richly endowed establishment under royal patronage. Its ceremonial had never been so elaborate or its services better attended. The ordinary Israelite, we may be sure, felt that he had the privilege of belonging to an uncommonly religious nation, which was properly rewarded for its piety by this unwonted prosperity. Amos had other standards of judgment, and the clarity and firmness with which he set the existing situation into the context of a loftier conception of religion gives him an outstanding place in the history of revelation.

To begin with, Amos held certain underlying convictions, or postulates, inherited from the past, and shared by most of his countrymen. He believed that between God and Israel there existed a specially close relation: they were His people, He their God. He also believed that the God of Israel was a 'living God', who acted powerfully in history; and he assumed that sooner or later the power and majesty of God would be finally revealed in a catastrophic historical event. On the 'Day of the Lord' the God of Israel would assert His authority over all nations.

So far, Amos kept step with the general beliefs of his time. Beyond that, he differed from them. God cared for Israel; true, but He cared more for righteousness. He was less concerned for the rights of His people than for the everlasting Right. If Israel defied the Right, God's judgment would fall upon Israel.

In his opening oration[1] he made a 'black list' of various neighbouring peoples, and pilloried their crimes. The Syrians would be punished for a ruthless massacre; the Philistines for playing jackal to Edom; the Phœnicians for a breach of treaty; the Edomites for attacking a kindred and friendly

1 Amos i. 3–ii. 16.

people; the Ammonites for slaughtering women and children in a wanton war of aggression; the Moabites for a brutal outrage upon the corpse of the conquered King of Edom. Here we can almost hear the general applause ('War-criminals, all of them; they deserve what is coming to them!'). But then the speech takes an unexpected turn.

> For three transgressions of *Israel*, yea for four,
> I will not turn away the punishment thereof:
>> Because they have sold the righteous for silver,
>> And the needy for a pair of shoes;
>> They trample the head of the poor into the dust of the earth,
>> And turn aside the way of the humble.

In short, to be God's people means bearing a special responsibility, rather than enjoying special privileges.

> You only have I known of all the families of the earth;
> *Therefore* I will visit upon you all your iniquities.[1]

No amount of 'religious observance' would make the slightest difference to the truth that in a world governed by a righteous, living God, national sin brings national disaster. Those who held it as an article of faith that on the 'Day of the Lord' Israel, being God's people, would triumph over all their enemies, were living in a fool's paradise. The goal of the divine purpose was not the victory of Israel, but the victory of Right.

> Woe unto you that desire the Day of the Lord!
> Wherefore would ye have the Day of the Lord?
>> It is darkness, and not light.[2]

For the moment, all seemed well, but the prophet was sensitively aware of the threatening international situation. The storm-clouds of Assyrian aggression were still distant, but in due time they would break, and bring God's judgement upon

1 Amos iii. 2.   2 Amos v. 18.

His rebellious people. There was only one thing that might even now avert the calamity:

> Hate the evil and love the good, and establish judgement in the gate; it may be that the Lord, the God of hosts, will be gracious unto the remnant of Joseph.[1]

Such was the burden of the prophecies of Amos in the middle of the eighth century B.C. History takes place within a moral order. In its process, rapid or slow, the connection between crime and calamity is not accidental. It is the judgement of the righteous and living God who is the Lord of history. In the light of subsequent developments we may conclude that Amos over-simplified the matter in some respects. But his declaration that history is a moral order under the rule of God is fundamental, and provided the starting-point for the whole prophetic movement—and indeed for any understanding of history and experience which does not reduce them to illusion.

We now pass to the second of the great prophets, Hosea, whom we may date some twenty or thirty years after Amos. Unlike him, he was a native of the more civilized northern kingdom, in which they both worked. We should judge him to have been a townsman, and less completely out of sympathy with the civilization of his time and country than the sheep-farmer of the Judaean wilderness. But he was as unsparing in his exposure of the corruptions of contemporary society, and he corroborated all that his predecessor had said about the inevitable judgement of God upon a rebellious people. He could not, however, stop there. He had a profound conviction that there was something in the relation between God and Israel that could not be finally destroyed by any faithlessness on their part, or by any fate that might befall them, however tragic.

1 Amos v. 15.

When Israel was a child, then I loved him,
　　And called my son out of Egypt....
I taught Ephraim to walk;
I took them on my arms;
　　But they knew not that I healed them.
I drew them with cords of a man,
　　With bands of love....
How shall I give thee up, Ephraim?
　　How shall I hand thee over, Israel?...
My heart is turned within me;
　　My compassions are kindled together.
I will not execute the fierceness of mine anger;
　　I will not return to destroy Ephraim.
For I am God and not man,
　　The Holy One of Israel in the midst of thee.[1]

God cannot let His people go. A community that has once stood in a vital relationship with God can never fall outside His care. Their sin will have its consequences. They lie under God's judgement and may be banished from His presence. But the relationship still holds. Hence Hosea saw, beyond the approaching disaster, the hope of reconciliation with God and new life for Israel.

He has thus enriched the conception of God's action in history as it was set forth by Amos. God is a God of mercy as well as of judgement. It cannot be said that Hosea entirely harmonized the two principles. But from now on the whole thought of the Old Testament moves between these two poles—the living God active in judgement, the same God active in mercy.

Before Hosea's work was ended, a still greater prophet came forward, this time in the southern kingdom. Isaiah of Jerusalem was a man of aristocratic birth and connections, the friend of kings. During most of his long life he stood near

1 Hosea xi. 1–9 (abridged).

to political circles in the capital, and he was acutely aware of the public problems, social and international, in which his country was involved. It was with direct reference to these problems that his religious teaching was developed.

Isaiah took over from his predecessors the fundamental conception of the righteous and living God, sovereign over history, active both in judgement and in mercy. Early in his career he witnessed the fulfilment of their forebodings of judgement in the downfall of the northern kingdom, and before long he had to face the probability of a similar fate for his own country. In the course of divine justice Judah had deserved no better than Israel. Isaiah's denunciations are as severe as those of Amos. But his conviction of the divine mercy is as sure as Hosea's.

He worked out the apparently contrary principles of the divine action into a kind of rudimentary philosophy of history. The nation as a body, he holds, lies under God's judgement, and must certainly perish, in default of some radical change. Yet God cannot abandon His people. However bad things may be, God will see to it that there are some, however few, among an apostate nation, who turn to Him with repentance and obedience, and out of them He will fashion His people anew. 'A remnant will turn':[1] this was the watchword in which Isaiah embodied his confidence in the future of the people of God.

When the Assyrian invasion seemed about to overwhelm the whole kingdom, Isaiah steadied king and people with the assurance that it was God's will to give them a respite during which they might turn to Him, and that for this purpose He would protect Jerusalem from imminent destruction. As we have seen, the Assyrian army suddenly, and inexplicably, evacuated its positions, and Jerusalem was saved. A generation which has spoken of the 'miracle of Dunkirk' need not

[1] Isaiah x. 16–23.

cavil at those who saw in the strange deliverance of Jerusalem a signal act of God's mercy to His people. At any rate the event did have, in history, precisely the meaning that the prophet attributed to it. It provided a respite, a space for repentance, before the final stroke fell; and so far as we can see, it was because of that respite that the Jewish people, unlike their kinsfolk of the north, survived the utter destruction of their state, and lived to hand on a great religious inheritance to the wider world.

Not that the escape from peril brought about any immediate or general reformation. Isaiah hardly expected it. But he was able to gather a small group of disciples, to whom he committed his teaching,[1] and in whom he saw the faithful 'remnant' of Israel—the 'seed', as he put it, of a holy people to come.[2]

Their loyalty was soon tested, for with political reaction under King Manasseh came religious reaction, and the prophetic party went underground. It emerged under Josiah, and inspired the reformation which he promoted. This was a brave attempt to put into effect by legislation the moral and religious principles which had been taught by Amos, Hosea, Isaiah, and other prophets of the previous century. The legislation is pretty well represented by the Book of Deuteronomy, or by the central portion of that book, which we may fairly describe as a prophetic revision of the ancient laws of Israel. It deserves careful study as an example of the application of religious principles to practical social needs, moulding a comparatively primitive order of society to the shape of justice and humanity.

Josiah's reformation however was almost stillborn. He became involved in the conflicts which ensued upon the fall of the Assyrian empire, and perished before he reached the age of forty, leaving no worthy successor. In the dark days

1 Isaiah viii. 16–17.   2 Isaiah vi. 13.

which followed, while the new Babylonian empire threatened the little nations ever more nearly, another of the great prophets came upon the scene. Jeremiah was the son of a country priest at a Judaean village. He is better known to us as an individual than any of his predecessors—possibly better than any other character in the Old Testament; for his book contains many chapters of personal confessions and autobiography. They show him as a lonely, tragic figure in a doomed society.[1]

He took up the prophetic tradition, and reaffirmed its central teachings in a situation which gave them urgent significance. For, estimating with clear insight the position of his country, he concluded that the final judgement which all the prophets had foreseen was now not only inevitable, but actually imminent. As time after time the Babylonian armies overran the country, as group after group of his countrymen disappeared into captivity, as the nation disintegrated into factions, and *morale* collapsed, he saw before his eyes the awful judgements of the living God.

When however his worst forebodings had come true, and his country lay in ruins, he had something further to say. God had acted in judgement; it remained for Him to act in mercy; for the people whom God had once loved He could not cease to love. They had violated all the terms upon which they had been recognized as His people; they had broken His 'covenant'. They had no longer any standing before Him, as of right. What then?

Behold, the days come, saith the Lord, that I will make a *new covenant* with the house of Israel and with the house of Judah; not like the covenant that I made with their fathers, in the day when I took them by the hand, to bring them out of the land of Egypt; which my covenant they brake, although

1 See especially Jeremiah xv. 10–11, 15–21, xx. 7–18.

I was an husband to them, saith the Lord. But this is the covenant that I will make with the house of Israel after those days, saith the Lord:

I will put my law in their inward parts,
    And in their hearts will I write it;
And I will be their God,
    And they shall be my people.
And they shall teach no more every man his neighbour,
    And every man his brother,
        Saying, 'Know the Lord';
For they shall all know me,
    From the least of them unto the greatest of them,
        saith the Lord;
For I will forgive their iniquity,
    And their sin will I remember no more.[1]

That is one of the epoch-making utterances in the history of religion. Jeremiah, we may recall, had in his youth been a witness of the reformation under Josiah, and had no doubt shared the enthusiasm with which it had been greeted by idealists of the time. It seemed that at last the aim for which good men had striven for a century and a half had been attained. The nation had returned to the Lord their God and sealed their repentance by the solemn acceptance of a high code of social morals such as the prophets had taught. But in the period of disillusion that followed he came to the conclusion (trite enough by now) that 'you cannot make people good by Act of Parliament'. It was not enough to write good laws into the statute-book. They must be written 'on the hearts' of men. In other words, the only adequate basis for right relations of men with God is an inward and personal understanding of His demands, an inward and personal response to them. It would not be true to say that Jeremiah first discovered the rôle of the individual in religion; for it is

1 Jeremiah xxxi. 31–34.

implicit in all prophetic teaching. But his clear emphasis upon it at the moment when the whole apparatus of public, 'institutional' religion had been swept away, was of the first importance for all subsequent development.

The scene now shifts from Judaea to Babylonia, where the deported Jews were living in exile. Among them was the prophet Ezekiel. Like Jeremiah, he was an hereditary priest, but from a *milieu* very different from the 'country parsonage' in which Jeremiah had grown up. He belonged (if one may continue with an inexact modern parallel) to the 'cathedral clergy' of the capital, and had the outlook and interests of a high ecclesiastic. He has been called, not inaptly, the 'prophet of reconstruction'. Much of his book is taken up with detailed schemes for the reorganization of the community, including plans for the rebuilding of the Temple, complete with measurements and specifications. But behind these somewhat tedious 'blue-prints' we discern a profound conviction that Israel had a future in spite of everything. There was nothing in the situation to support such a belief. We might have dismissed Ezekiel's projects of reconstruction as no better than 'wishful thinking' if the reconstruction had not in course of time actually come about (though not precisely as he had imagined it). His grounds for believing in it were not derived from a calculation of the probabilities of the situation, but from the prophetic faith in God's indestructible loyalty to His people, in face of their disloyalty to Him. In spite of appearances, God would certainly have mercy upon Israel, and it was for them to be ready for Him.

Ezekiel had taken to heart Jeremiah's teaching about the essential rôle of the individual in the 'new covenant'. Indeed, in his anxiety to press home to each man's conscience his individual responsibility before God, he sometimes overstates his case, without sufficiently allowing for the undoubted influence of heredity and environment upon individual character and destiny.[1] But if we take Ezekiel's teaching as a whole we shall not suspect him of the kind of pure individualism in religion which has become familiar in the modern world. We may put it that he conceives social renewal in terms of individual conversion. The real cause of such renewal lies in the mercy of God, which calls for man's individual response.

In a famous chapter[2] he has given us an imaginative picture of the resurrection of a nation. He imagines himself standing on an old battlefield, littered with the whitening bones of the slain. At the word of God the scattered bones come together and clothe themselves with flesh and skin, and at the blast of a great wind (which is the breath, or spirit, of God) the dead bodies come alive, 'an exceeding great army'. 'These bones', he adds in explanation, 'are the whole house of Israel. Behold, they say, "Our bones are dried up and our hope is lost".... Thus saith the Lord God, Behold I will open your graves, and cause you to come up out of your graves, O my people...and I will put my spirit in you, and ye shall live.'

The restoration of Israel, in fact, will have the character of a resurrection from the dead. The implication is that no human situation is too desperate to be retrieved by the grace of God, who works in history in His own incalculable ways and at His own time. In that faith the Jewish exiles faced the dark future.

Nearly half a century passed by after the destruction of Jerusalem. A new generation arose. Then the liberal policy of Cyrus, King of Persia, opened the way for a return to Palestine. Many of the exiles had settled down very comfortably and had no appetite for the difficulties of life in a ruined city and an impoverished and unfamiliar countryside. A comparatively small group saw in the king's edict the sign

1 Ezekiel xviii.   2 Ezekiel xxxvii. 1–14.

for which they had waited. It was the Lord's doing: the time had come for the restoration of Israel. They were encouraged and inspired by one of the greatest of all the prophets, whose name, however, we do not know. His writings have come down to us bound together with the prophecies of Isaiah of Jerusalem, two centuries earlier, and some other material, under the general title, 'The Book of Isaiah'. Chapters xl–lv of that book contain the prophecies of the great Anonymous of the Exile, which are often referred to, conveniently though inaccurately, as those of the 'Second Isaiah'.

The writer who goes under this name has left us some of the most magnificent poetry in the Bible—poetry which is largely free from the archaic obscurity of some of the earlier prophets, and can be enjoyed for the power and range of its imagery and its richly embroidered language, as well as for the sublimity of its thought, which touches, probably, the highest level reached anywhere in the Old Testament. His themes are the ultimate themes of all religious thought—the kingdom and the power and the glory of God, the wonder and mystery of His ways with men. In the name of this God he proclaims the restoration of Israel, and summons the exiles to return and enter upon their inheritance, with all its benefits and responsibilities.

> How beautiful upon the mountains are the feet of him
>   That bringeth good tidings,
>   That publisheth peace,
>   That bringeth good tidings of good,
>   That publisheth salvation;
> That saith unto Zion, 'Thy God reigneth!' . . .
>
> Break forth into joy,
>   Sing together, ye waste places of Jerusalem;
> For the Lord hath comforted His people;
>   He hath redeemed Jerusalem.

The Lord hath made bare His holy arm in the eyes of all
the nations;
And all the ends of the earth shall see the salvation of
our God.

Depart ye, depart ye!
Go ye out from thence!...
Ye shall not go out in haste,
Neither shall ye go by flight;
For the Lord shall go before you;
And the God of Israel shall be your rearguard.[1]

Such was the mood in which the repatriated exiles faced
the problems of reconstruction. The community which they
organized was on a very small scale. It was politically insignificant; its territory was no larger than an English county;
it had no military power at all, and only the scantiest economic
resources. But it became the centre of a widely-dispersed
religious commonwealth which was, as we have seen, a
unique form of social structure, and has had an incalculable
influence in history. It is not too much to say that if this
handful of devoted and practical men had not faced and carried
through their almost hopeless task the world would never have
seen three of the most potent factors in all subsequent history
(potent whether for good or ill): international Judaism, the
Christian Church, and Islam. In the Jews' Return from
Exile, then, we have an event which, though its scale was so
minute as to be almost invisible on a chart of world-history,
was, on any showing, a decisive turning-point, of which the
historian must take serious account.

There is a problem here. Why did the Jewish nation sur-
vive at all, when so many of the smaller nations of antiquity
sooner or later lost their identity in the melting-pot of the
great empires of the Middle East? Few nations were to all
appearance more effectively put down: exhausted by suc-

1 Isaiah lii. 7–12 (abridged).

cessive defeats in war, reduced to a mere remnant, deported to distant countries, subjected to the long-continued domination of alien and highly civilized Great Powers. And yet they survived, reconstructed their community, and handed down a continuous and developing tradition which exerted a creative influence upon the whole of subsequent history. Why was it? The only answer that explains the facts is that the prophets of the two great centuries worked out a particular interpretation of the course of history, and induced their people to accept it, at least in sufficient numbers to give a new direction to their history for the future.

That is, however, not how the prophets themselves would have put it. They were not philosophers, constructing a speculative theory from their observation of events. What they said was 'Thus saith the Lord'. They firmly believed that God spoke to them (spoke to the inward ear, the spiritual sense). He spoke to them out of the events which they experienced. The interpretation of history which they offered was not invented by process of thought; it was the meaning which they experienced in the events, when their minds were opened to God as well as open to the impact of outward facts. Thus the prophetic interpretation of history, and the impetus and direction which that interpretation gave to subsequent history, were alike the Word of God to men.

Nowhere are the springs of prophecy more clearly and impressively disclosed than in the account which Isaiah gives of the experience which made him a prophet, in the sixth chapter of his book. It takes the form of a 'vision'. The oriental imagery in which it is clothed is no doubt strange to a modern western mind. It must be read with the imagination awake (as the Bible, and all great religious literature, always should be read). Imagine, then, the young courtier, deeply concerned with the social and political problems of his country, which is faced by a 'demise of the crown' at a time of crisis in international affairs; concerned with these problems, but at a level deeper than that of ordinary political discussion. He has been attending at worship in the Temple, and remains there in meditation, his eyes upon the still smoking altar, and the bizarre carved figures of supernatural beings which we know to have adorned the building. And now listen to him:[1]

In the year that King Uzziah died, I saw the Lord, sitting upon a throne, high and lifted up; and his train filled the Temple. About him stood the seraphim...and one cried to another and said,

'Holy, holy, holy is the Lord of hosts;
The whole earth is full of his glory.'

And the foundations of the thresholds were moved at the voice of him that cried, and the house was filled with smoke. Then said I,

'Woe is me! for I am undone;
Because I am a man of unclean lips,
And I dwell in the midst of a people of unclean lips;
For mine eyes have seen the King,
The Lord of hosts.'

Then flew one of the seraphim unto me, having a live coal in his hand, which he had taken with the tongs from off the altar; and he touched my mouth with it, and said,

'Lo this hath touched thy lips;
And thine iniquity is taken away,
And thy sin purged.'

And I heard the voice of the Lord, saying,

'Whom shall I send,
And who will go for us?'

Then I said,

'Here am I; send me.'

Surely that authenticates itself as a basic personal experience. And observe that there is in it already everything which is

[1] Isaiah vi. 1–8.

essential to the prophetic interpretation of history. There is the sense of the majesty and holiness of the eternal God, as the fundamental fact of all. There is man in the presence of God, both judged and pardoned. There is the call of God, and man's response. Isaiah and his compeers all said, 'That is the meaning of history: it is God confronting man in judgement and mercy, and challenging him with a call, to which he must respond'. It was because they saw the meaning of history in that sense, and induced a sufficient number of people to accept it, that history took the shape it did. As we have seen, there is a continuous chain of events, and of the understanding of events, from the emergence of Isaiah as a prophet to the reconstitution of the Jewish community in the sixth century, which had such momentous results for the history of succeeding centuries.

I have dealt with the prophetic period in some detail, because it supplies the clue to the understanding of the Old Testament as a whole. As we have seen, the books of the Old Testament, in their complete form, were composed in the prophetic period or later, and bear the stamp of the prophets upon them. The historical books, for example (Judges, Samuel and Kings, which the Jews call, not inaptly, 'the former prophets'), were 'written up', from earlier records, by followers of the prophets; and their influence was felt in the compilation of the books from Genesis to Joshua. They undertook the writing of the history of Israel in order to show the meaning that was in it, according to the teaching of the prophets. We shall now consider more briefly some of the earlier parts of the history, using the clue provided by the prophetic literature.

To begin with, the prophets always show themselves aware that what they are saying is not altogether new. There have been revelations of God in history before their time. In particular, they frequently call to mind how God 'brought up Israel out of the land of Egypt'. The Exodus from Egypt is for them a decisive act of the living God in past history, and makes a kind of fixed point of reference for all discussions of His ways with His people.

Of the events of the Exodus we have no written account which is anything like contemporary. The story has come down to us richly overlaid with legend. Legend, however, properly treated, is one of the most important sources of historical knowledge. The poems of Homer, containing the immortal legends of the Trojan War, were in my schooldays put down as pure fiction. Nowadays, though no one doubts that the dramatic detail of the Flight of Helen, the Wrath of Achilles, and the rest, is imaginary, the poems are treated as valuable sources of evidence for the history of Greece and neighbouring lands shortly before 1000 B.C. Even our own Arthurian legends, I observe, are now treated seriously by quite serious historians, when they are seeking for light upon the dark age of Britain.

The fact is that legend is the form which the memory of events assumes in what are called 'heroic ages'. These are formative periods when some new civilization or social order is shaping itself, usually out of the confused turmoil brought about by great folk-migrations. In such periods history is highly dynamic. There is neither stability nor ordered progress: all is fluid. The exigencies of the time throw up outstanding leaders, whose exploits loom larger than human in the imagination of their followers and successors. The settled conditions necessary for the writing of sober history are altogether absent; yet the facts imprint themselves deeply upon folk-memory, and are handed down in the characteristic form of heroic legends. The period from the Exodus to the Judges has much of the character of an heroic age of Israel; and Moses is its supreme hero.

The principal external facts can be told shortly. Apparently certain Hebrew-speaking clans, inhabiting the borderlands of Egypt as serfs of the Egyptian crown, were driven by increasing oppression to throw off their servile bonds and take to a nomadic life. They found courage for this decisive step through the inspiration of a great leader, who led them into the wilderness. There he induced them to accept the rudiments of a legal code and a religious system, through which they were disciplined and brought into conscious political unity, with the potentiality of developing in course of time into a nation. Invigorated by these experiences, they broke into Palestine and carved out territories for themselves at the expense of the settled and civilized population.

The story has its centre in the heroic leader Moses. With the later prophets in our minds, we can recognize in him a man of prophetic mould, though of a more primitive type. Like Isaiah and the others, he was called by God. While keeping sheep, we are told, he heard a voice addressing him out of the heart of a flame: 'Put off thy shoes from off thy feet, for the place whereon thou standest is holy ground.' 'And Moses' (the story continues) 'hid his face, for he was afraid to look upon God.' The voice proceeds: 'I have surely seen the affliction of my people which are in Egypt, and have heard their cry by reason of their taskmasters; for I know their sorrows. . . . Come now therefore, and I will send thee unto Pharaoh, that thou mayst bring forth my people the children of Israel out of Egypt.'[1] After some resistance, Moses accepts the commission; and the whole plot is set in motion. Read the story in all its detail in the third chapter of Exodus.

We can recognize, under the legendary form, the same kind of personal experience as that described in the classical passage in Isaiah. There is the overpowering sense of the mystery and majesty of God, the human shrinking from the

[1] See Exodus iii. 1–10.

encounter, and the final yielding to the divine imperative which sets the task. As with the prophets, the call is an intensely personal experience, but has an immediate reference to the needs and the destiny of a people. It is by the Word of God, thus delivered intimately to His servant, that the people are nerved for their great adventure. It is by His providence that they cross the Red Sea in safety and escape from the Egyptian host (as it was by His providence that Jerusalem was later to be saved from the Assyrians). The laws which Moses induces them to accept are the terms of His covenant, by which they become the people of their God. The entire story is told as a story of God's action in history. It was because these events were so understood, that the little kingdoms of Israel and Judah, which grew out of the invasion of Palestine, made a fertile ground for the later prophetic teaching about God's revelation in history.

The stories of the Exodus and the conquest of Palestine presuppose a remoter background of events. 'The Lord which brought thee up out of the land of Egypt' is also 'the God of thy fathers, the God of Abraham, of Isaac and of Jacob.'[1] Most nations possess legends of their remote ancestors. The ancestry to which the Israelites of the prophetic period laid claim was not distinguished, and therefore the more credible. 'A wandering Syrian was my father, and he went down to Egypt and sojourned there, few in number.'[2] So runs the liturgy for Harvest Festival in Deuteronomy. In other words, the founders of the Hebrew race to which Israel belonged were nomads of Syrian extraction, who migrated southward to Egypt. The names given to these primeval wanderers are Abraham, Isaac and Jacob. Their traditional stories, handed down from mouth to mouth through many generations, are in the Book of Genesis. They have much of the universal

1 Exodus iii. 15.   2 Deuteronomy xxvi. 5.

quality of folk-tales. Often, in reading them, we seem to be moving in a timeless world outside history, the world of 'once upon a time'.

Yet there is history behind them. Their picture of nomadic existence in the debatable lands between the great civilizations of the Nile and the Euphrates is life-like and convincing. These 'wandering Syrians' were not primitive nomads. They had, it appears, broken away at an early date from the settled civilization of Mesopotamia. The sophisticated brilliance of that ancient civilization astonished those who a few years ago visited the London exhibition of works of art discovered by excavation at Ur of the Chaldees, Abraham's own city. The moment when the founders of the Hebrew race separated themselves from it, and began their migrations was, in view of all that followed from it, a turning-point in history, though at the time there was nothing in it to attract attention.

We should like to know what combination of circumstances—political, economic, or military—led them to the decision; but there is no record. The biblical story confines itself to the simple statement that Abraham heard the call of God. 'The Lord said unto Abraham, "Get thee out of thy country, and from thy kindred, and from thy father's house, unto the land that I will show thee"': [1] upon which a writer of the New Testament fitly comments, 'By faith Abraham, when he was called, obeyed,...and he went out, not knowing whither he went'.[2] The response to a compelling inward call shows itself characteristically in this spirit of detachment, this readiness to cut loose and venture upon the unknown. We have learned from the prophets how the Word of God makes history when it comes to a man as the meaning of the facts of his experience, and through his response gives a new direction to events. Here at the begin-

[1] Genesis xii. 1. The clan is already away from Ur, but still in the Euphrates basin, when the call comes.   [2] Hebrews xi. 8.

ning of the Bible story we recognize the prophetic pattern at its simplest.

I have selected these three episodes from the story of the Old Testament—the call of Abraham, the exodus from Egypt, and the long-drawn struggle which ended in the Babylonian captivity and the restoration—because they mark critical points in the movement of history in which we are invited to recognize the revelation of God in action, and they indicate the pattern to which the history as a whole conforms.

This brings us down to the end of the sixth century B.C. The five centuries which followed were a period of great literary activity, during which the bulk of the books of the Old Testament and the Apocrypha took shape (though often on the basis of earlier materials). Of the events of the period the literature has little to say, in comparison with the copious records of the preceding five centuries.

This is at first sight surprising. Events of great consequence for the world took place in these centuries: the fall of the Persian empire; the conquests of Alexander the Great and their dissolution after his death; the long struggles between the Greek dynasties of Syria and of Egypt; and the advance of Rome as residuary legatee of them all. The tiny dependent state of Judaea was inevitably drawn into these events, but their impact upon the Jewish mind was not such as to raise great spiritual issues, or to provoke new understanding of the ways of God with men.

There is one notable exception which, as they say, 'proves the rule'. In the second century B.C. the Greek monarch of Syria, Antiochus Epiphanes, set out to bring his miscellaneous empire into a greater measure of cultural uniformity (the now familiar policy of *Gleichschaltung*); and in furtherance of this policy he attempted to enforce upon his Jewish subjects conformity with the religious observances of the state.

The Jews, who had shown no great reluctance to speak Greek or to follow many of the manners and customs of their fellow-subjects, drew the line when loyalty to their religion was involved. Persecution followed, and this provoked a rebellion, which was partly religious and partly nationalist, under the leadership of a family of whom the heroic Judas Maccabaeus was the chief. Under him and his successors the Jews gained political independence for a time. This episode is recorded in full in the apocryphal books of Maccabees, and it has left deep traces upon other literature of the period, some of which we shall notice presently.[1] At this one point history was felt to disclose once again something of the compelling spiritual significance which it had possessed for the prophets, though at a lower level of intensity.

The significance of the post-exilic period, however, resides less in external events than in the process by which the life of the Jewish community was built up internally. It was the period when the teachings of the prophets, accepted in their time by a mere handful, seeped into the blood and bones of the people. A real and sustained effort was made to reconstruct the whole social order upon the basis of the Law of God, not only by giving it statutory force, but by 'writing it on the heart', so far as this could be done by positive instruction and through the ordinances of public worship.

The ancient laws of Israel, some of them going back to very remote antiquity indeed, were collected, codified and annotated. We have the results in the so-called Pentateuch, or Five Books of Moses (Genesis to Deuteronomy), which received their present shape about the fourth century B.C. Similarly, the works of the prophets were collected, arranged, and edited for the use of later generations. The historical records of earlier times received a good deal of reshaping, again with a view to enforcing the teaching of the prophets

1 See pp. 61–62.

rather than for purely historical purposes. (Aristotle would have approved: he held that history is 'the teaching of philosophy by examples'.) At the same time they worked out a most elaborate liturgy for the Temple—a liturgy designed to preserve the immemorial traditions of Israelite worship, while eliminating those pagan elements which had clung to it down to the Exile, and adapting it to the expression of the loftiest ideas of the prophetic religion. The Book of Psalms seems to have been the hymn-book of the Temple liturgy—a book, quite literally, of 'hymns ancient and modern', since it contains poems of the period of the monarchy (possibly, as some believe, as old as David), and others composed as late as the third century or even (as some suppose) the second century B.C.

Within the framework of law and liturgy there went on a process of what we should call 'religious education'. It is principally represented in the literature of the period by the so-called 'Wisdom' books. Among these are the Book of Proverbs and the apocryphal Ecclesiasticus, full of wise saws and simple pieties. These are addressed to a more or less 'popular' audience. On a far higher level, intellectually and spiritually, is that very noble philosophical poem called the Wisdom of Solomon, and that still nobler monument of ancient Hebrew thought, the Book of Job, a dramatic dialogue in splendid and sonorous verse upon the theme of suffering and its place in a providential order.

While however the life of the community was thus being reconstructed under the inspiration of the prophetic faith, we trace a growing sense of something incomplete or inconclusive about the interpretation of history upon which it all rested. The prophets had declared that history takes place within a moral order determined by the will of God. Corporate sin and corporate calamity are organically connected, and faithfulness to the law of God will in the long run bring a blessing.

No biblical writer seriously intends to deny that fundamental position. But to verify it in detail through the facts of actual experience was not too easy. When the attempt was made to apply it to individual destiny (which was scarcely in the minds of the earlier prophets), in the sense that the wicked are punished by misfortune and the good rewarded by prosperity, it appeared palpably untrue, not only to the sceptical author of Ecclesiastes, but also to the far profounder poet of the Book of Job. But even in the corporate application which was originally intended, the principle became increasingly difficult to maintain, as century after century passed, and the Jewish people found themselves in a worsening situation of poverty and oppression, in spite of their endeavours to keep the law of God.

Jewish thought gradually moved to a position in which the prophetic doctrine was reaffirmed, upon a clearly expressed condition. History is indeed a moral order, in which judgements of the living God take effect; but this view cannot be fully verified upon the plane of history as we know it, since there is an irreducible element of tragedy in human affairs. It can be maintained upon the assumption that the pattern of history, always incomplete within our present experience, will finally be completed. Somehow, somewhere, at some time, history will reach a climax, in which the purpose of God in all history will be conclusively exhibited, and His last word spoken. This doctrine (which is often referred to as 'eschatology', meaning a doctrine about the End) is principally embodied in a new type of literature which was developed in our period, commonly called the 'apocalypse' (or 'revelation').

The most typical example of apocalyptic writing in the Old Testament is to be found in the Book of Daniel. It seems clear that this work was produced during the persecution under Antiochus Epiphanes, to which I have already referred. The acute sufferings of that time brought to a head the misgivings about God's providence in history which had been aroused by long-continued misfortunes and disappointments; for these sufferings not only fell upon a people which had made sincere and persistent efforts to observe the law of God in its corporate life, but they fell most heavily upon the best members of the community. How could it be said that history was the instrument of God's judgement?

In answer to this difficulty the author of the Book of Daniel puts forward a philosophy of history which may be shortly stated thus. In this present age (history as we know it) God has, for reasons best known to Himself, allowed relative freedom of action to the powers of this world, which often act in opposition to His will, and cause suffering to those who keep His law. But even so, 'the Most High ruleth in the kingdom of men';[1] the sufferings of the righteous serve not only to test the loyalty of His servants and to call out their courage, but in some inscrutable way as preparation for the final *dénouement* of history. When the time is ripe, God will act with absolute power, and set up a kingdom of righteousness which will endure for ever.

After the manner usual in apocalypses, this doctrine is presented in the form of symbolic pictures, or 'visions'. In particular, there are two visions which run parallel and are complementary to one another. In the first,[2] there is a monstrous idol, which stands for all the evil empires of heathendom. It is made out of varied materials, for the tyrannies that oppress the human spirit differ among themselves, but all make up one power of evil. (We could add a few to the list of those known in the second century B.C.) Thereupon a stone 'cut out of the mountain without hands' strikes the image, and it falls apart:

1 Daniel iv. 17, 25.   2 Daniel ii. 31–45.

Then was the iron, the clay, the brass, the silver and the gold, broken in pieces together, and became like the chaff of the summer threshing-floors; and the wind carried them away, that no place was found for them; and the stone that smote the image became a great mountain, and filled the whole earth.

No human hands (he means) prepare the weapon by which the power of evil in the world will ultimately be overthrown: it is the act of God alone, whose kingdom will then be effective over all creation.

In the second vision,[1] there is a procession of weird beasts— a winged lion, a bear, a winged leopard, and a ghastly thing of indescribable shape and appalling ferocity. These beasts stand, once again, for the evil world-powers, embodied in history as successive empires. The monsters rage and ramp; but over against them sits enthroned the 'Ancient of Days' (the eternal God); and 'the judgement was set and the books were opened'. The beasts receive their doom, and pass from the scene: the powers of evil are overthrown, not by any human virtue or strength, but by the presence and power of the living God.

But now a new character appears on the scene:

Behold there came with the clouds of heaven one like unto a son of man [i.e. a manlike figure, in contrast to the beasts]; and he came even to the Ancient of Days, and they brought him near before Him. And there was given him dominion, and glory, and a kingdom, that all the peoples, nations, and languages should serve him: his dominion is an everlasting dominion, and his kingdom that which shall not be destroyed.

The 'son of man', it is explained, stands for 'the people of the saints of the Most High'. That is to say, God's final

1 Daniel vii.

sovereignty is to be realized in and through a community wholly conformed to His will, the true people of God at last.

The book ends with the haunting words: 'Blessed is he that waiteth.... But go thou thy way till the end be: for thou shalt rest, and shalt stand in thy lot at the end of the days.'[1] Upon this note the Old Testament may be said to end: the confused pattern of world-history will be completed by the Word of God; wait upon Him and be prepared.

1 Daniel xii. 12–13.

CHAPTER IV

THE NEW TESTAMENT

Pursuing the historical line of approach which we have followed hitherto, we observe that the writings of the New Testament are concerned with the emergence of an historical community of a new type: the Christian Church.

Beginning as an insignificant group within Judaism, in a decade it was breaking bounds, and showed itself in principle 'catholic' or universal. In the space of one generation it was already strong enough in Rome, the metropolis of world-empire, to draw upon itself the unwelcome attention of the government. In two centuries it had become a vast international corporation, challenging the power of the empire, which tried to destroy it, but had to acknowledge defeat. In little more than three centuries the empire was absorbed in Christendom, which was to be the framework for mediaeval civilization. In modern times the Church is still a significant factor in world-history—significant positively and negatively, by way of action and reaction—and significant now over a wider area than ever before, in spite of serious set-backs in regions where it has been long established. It follows that the emergence of the Church in the first century is an historical phenomenon of first-rate importance.

Like many new movements, Christianity exhibits in its earliest history three successive stages: expansion, conflict, consolidation. The writings of the New Testament connect themselves naturally with these three stages, which may serve to provide a rough chronological scheme.

1. The first stage, that of expansion, began shortly after the death of Jesus Christ at Jerusalem in the reign of Tiberius,

and went on without interruption for about thirty years. In the space of a single generation Christian communities were established in most of the eastern provinces of the Roman empire, and as far west as Italy: a remarkable achievement for a society which started with a handful of humble folk from the small towns of a petty 'native state'.[1] Geographical extension was accompanied by an intensive development which was at least as remarkable. During these few years the foundations were laid, by bold and imaginative thinking, for the massive structure of Christian theology and philosophy which later generations were to build.

This first stage is directly represented by the Epistles of Paul, the greatest of all early Christian missionaries and theologians. The majority of them were written during the most active part of his career, and are full of the enthusiasm, optimism and expansive energy which belonged to a period of spiritual adventure. The same period is indirectly reflected in the Acts of the Apostles, which, though written later,

---

[1] Galilee under Herod Antipas had a status similar to that of a small Indian state under the British Raj. It was thriving and populous, but culturally a backwater. The first followers of Jesus, so far as our scanty information goes, were neither 'Galilaean peasants' nor members of the 'proletariate'. Those of whom we know anything seem rather to have been *petits bourgeois*: four of them were 'partners' in a small family firm owning and operating fishing-boats and employing labour (Luke v. 1–11); one had been a minor civil servant (Mark ii. 14). None of them, doubtless, had been well-to-do, but the poverty in which we find them living was voluntarily chosen for the sake of a cause. They all had something to lose when they followed Jesus (Mark x. 28). By metropolitan standards they, like their Master, were 'uneducated'; but we need not take this piece of intellectual snobbery too seriously (John vii. 15; Acts iv. 13). So much should be said to guard against exaggeration. It remains that as pioneers of a movement which was to cover half the Roman world in a generation the first Christians started with few advantages.

preserves the traditions, and much of the spirit, of the early days.

2. The end of the first period may be fixed at the point where expansion was checked (temporarily) by the repressive action of the Roman government under Nero in the winter of A.D. 64/5. There had been a disastrous fire in the city of Rome. The story got about that the Emperor, who (it was believed) had fiddled while Rome was burning, had deliberately caused the fire, which was at any rate convenient for his town-planning schemes. The government searched for a scapegoat (like the Nazis after the Reichstag fire of 1933). They fixed upon the Christians. The Church was, in effect, outlawed, and its members hunted down with the greatest brutality.

For thirty years or so, the Christians, though not continually under persecution, were made painfully aware that they held a most precarious footing in a hostile society. The typical literature of the time has little of the buoyancy of the first period. It is constantly preoccupied with the necessity of fortitude and endurance. Such are the First Epistle of Peter, the Epistle to the Hebrews, and the Revelation of John. While the two former speak as if really severe persecution were a new experience, the last of the three speaks as if martyrdom was the normal expectation of a Christian. It was written towards the close of our period, when active persecution had flared up afresh under the Emperor Domitian.

It was natural enough that the Church, thus brought to bay, should pause to gather inspiration and confidence from the memories of its Founder, and since the inevitable disappearance of the first generation of witnesses was now being greatly accelerated by the persecution, it became important that these memories should be perpetuated in writing. The first attempt at a connected account of the career of Jesus Christ, so far as we know, was the Gospel according to

Mark, though short collections of His sayings, and probably parts of His story, were already in writing for use in the missionary work of the Church. Mark composed his Gospel, it appears, in the first years of persecution, and the atmosphere of the time betrays itself in his emphasis upon the example of Christ's sufferings, and upon the call to 'take up the cross and follow'.

The Gospels according to Matthew and Luke appeared some years later, but both, perhaps, before the death of Domitian. The former is based upon the work of Mark, and it retains the note of a time of sufferings. But its main purpose is to be recognized in the comprehensive and systematic account which it gives of the teaching of Jesus Christ. It thus provided a firm basis for the internal consolidation of the life of the Christian community which was now seen more than ever to be necessary. The Gospel according to Luke has a different orientation. It is really the first part, or volume, of a work dealing with the origins of Christianity, the second volume being the Acts of the Apostles. The whole work is dedicated to a friendly official, the 'most excellent Theophilus'. The author is in fact appealing, over the heads of the agents of persecution, to intelligent and well-disposed persons in Graeco-Roman society, in the belief that accurate information about the origins, aims and principles of the Christian Church would do much to disarm the hostility under which it suffered.

3. The murder of the Emperor Domitian in A.D. 96 brought to the throne a succession of humane and enlightened rulers who, though they did not reverse the decision which made the Church, in principle, an illegal society, did much, by administrative action, to relieve its situation. In New Testament writings after this date we hear little of actual persecution. Taught by experience, the Church was by now well aware of the necessity to consolidate its communal life, in order

both to present a firmly united front to a hostile world, and to ensure the integrity of its membership in faith and morals. Hence the literature of this period is much concerned with the promotion of order and discipline, and the correction of irregularities of belief and practice. Such are the 'Pastoral Epistles' to Timothy and Titus,[1] the 'General Epistles' of John and Jude, and the so-called Second Epistle of Peter, which is probably the latest work in the New Testament, not much earlier than the middle of the second century.

While this work of internal consolidation went on, fresh attempts were made to interpret the meaning of the faith to outsiders. In particular, the author of the Fourth Gospel, whose book is to be dated within a few years on either side of A.D. 100, wrote for a public familiar, as he was himself, with much of the best religious thought of the time in non-Christian circles. For such a public he retold the Gospel story in terms which would enable them to understand its deeper meanings, and win their assent. He succeeded in his aim. During the centuries immediately following, the subtle and powerful Greek intellect was enlisted in the task of constructing a Christian theology largely under the influence of the 'Johannine' interpretation of the Gospel.

Such is the general sequence of the New Testament writings. The time-factor, however, is less important here than in the Old Testament. The whole literature falls within a century or less. While in the Old Testament we have the long process of over a thousand years, punctuated by a series of well-marked crises, the New Testament presents one supreme crisis alone. The thought of all its writers, with all

1 It seems likely that these epistles, in their present form, were composed round about A.D. 100, partly out of shorter letters treasured as relics of the great apostle, and partly out of the oral tradition of his teaching and practice.

their diversity, is concentrated intensely upon the events related in the Gospels, and their significance.

The history of the Old Testament, as we have traced it, consists of alternating phases of crisis and development, through which Israel is shaped, under the divine providence, into a people of God. All through, but notably in the latest phase, there is a sense of inconclusiveness and a forward reference. Always Israel is the people of God, and at the same time is *not yet* the people of God in the fullest sense. The ideal attributes which the prophets applied to Israel are finally understood to await realization in an age yet to come, when God will intervene with a mighty hand to fulfil His purpose. The writers of the New Testament take up these ideal attributes and apply them to the Church. The Church is the 'Israel of God'.[1] It is a 'people for God's own possession',[2] whose members are 'kings and priests to God'.[3] It is Isaiah's righteous Remnant,[4] Jeremiah's people of the New Covenant,[5] Ezekiel's new Israel risen from the dead,[6] the 'ransomed' (liberated) people of the Second Isaiah,[7] Daniel's 'people of the saints of the Most High'.[8] This is not enthusiastic rhetoric. It is a deliberate re-application of prophetic language. It amounts to an assertion that the people of God has now passed through its supreme crisis, and reached its complete and final form.

1 Galatians vi. 16.
2 I Peter ii. 9.   3 Revelation i. 6.
4 Isaiah x. 22–23, quoted Romans ix. 27–28.
5 Jeremiah xxxi. 31–34, quoted at length Hebrews viii. 8–12; cf. II Corinthians iii. 4–18.
6 Ephesians ii. 4–10; Romans viii. 9–11, etc.
7 Romans iii. 24; I Corinthians i. 30–31, etc.
8 'The saints' is one of the recurrent designations of Christians, meaning, not persons of perfect character, but members of a community consecrated to God, e.g. I Corinthians i. 2, iii. 17, cf. Acts xx. 32.

Paul puts the matter very clearly when he draws the picture of a boy born heir to a great estate.[1] The estate is his, inalienably, by virtue of his father's will. But during his minority he has no enjoyment of his property. He is 'under tutors and governors', who keep him strictly in leading-strings. He is little better off than a slave. But when he comes of age, he enters into full possession of all that his father designed for him. Just so, the people of God is heir to a spiritual estate, which may be characterized sufficiently for our present purpose as the 'justice, peace and happiness' which are the marks of the Kingdom of God.[2] This estate was granted in principle to Abraham, and belonged in the purpose of God to the nation which Abraham founded. But all down the long centuries the heir failed to enjoy possession. His liberty was restricted; 'justice, peace and happiness' visited him only in tantalizing glimpses; the Kingdom of God he saw only in visions of the future. But now, the heir is of age: the estate is his in full possession. The Kingdom of God is here. All that God designed for His people is available within the Church of Christ.

This is strong language. If we are to take it as seriously as it was meant, we must be clear just what it affirms and what it does not.

First, these claims are not made for individual members of the Church, each of whom must say with Paul, 'I count not myself to have apprehended...but I press toward the mark'.[3] They are made for the Church as a body.

Secondly, they are not made for the Church so far as it is an exclusive body with a limited membership; but for the Church as 'catholic' or universal, ideally identified with the whole human race as 'redeemed' through Christ. Universality of membership was the most obvious mark of the Christian

---

1 Galatians iii. 23–iv. 7. 2 Romans xiv. 17.
3 Philippians iii. 13–14.

Church as compared with the Jewish Dispersion. After some preliminary hesitation, it was accepted irreversibly as an essential principle of Christianity: 'there is neither Jew nor Greek, circumcision nor uncircumcision, barbarian, Scythian, slave or free'.[1] For Paul, the union of those irreconcilables—Jew and Gentile—in the one body was a sure pledge of the ultimate unity of all mankind in the fulfilment of God's eternal purpose.[2] This unity of all mankind in Christ is what the Church means.

Thirdly, the attributes of the people of God (its liberty, righteousness, holiness and glory) do not belong primarily or of right either to individual Christians, or to the sum of all Christians at any one moment, or even to the whole of redeemed humanity in all ages. They are primarily attributes of Christ, shared by Him with those who depend upon Him. The Church is heir to the Kingdom of God, only because it is 'in Christ', who is the real Son and Heir of the eternal Father. Christ is a 'representative personality', who in some sort includes in Himself the whole people of God, and acts on their behalf. When Paul echoes Ezekiel's memorable language about Israel being raised from the dead by the breath of God, what he says is that we are dead *with Christ* and raised with Him.[3] In other words, it is in Christ, in what He did and suffered on our behalf, that the renewal of God's people is accomplished. The Church as a body is 'the Body of Christ';[4] its members are 'members of Christ'.[5] In the Gospels, Jesus often speaks of Himself as 'The Son of Man'. This title recalls the 'one like a son of man' who in Daniel's vision stood for 'the people of the saints of the Most High', implying once

---

1 Colossians iii. 11; Galatians iii. 28.
2 Ephesians ii. 11–22.
3 Colossians ii. 11, 12, iii. 1–4.   4 Ephesians i. 22–23.
5 I Corinthians xii. 27, vi. 15; Ephesians v. 30. Upon this idea of the Church see further, chap. VII, pp. 155–157.

again the 'solidarity' of the Church in and with Christ, and His 'representative' action on its behalf. This is in fact a large part of the meaning of the title 'Christ' or 'Messiah', as it is used in the New Testament.

This brings us to a notable difference between the Old Testament and the New. The Old Testament recounts episodes in the history of the people of Israel, interpreted and directed through prophetic men. The story is about a community; the interpretation comes through individual insight. In the New Testament the story is no longer, primarily, about a community, but about a Person. It is the story of Jesus, who acts and suffers as 'Messiah', as representative of the people of God, and so, secondarily and derivatively, it is the story of the Church as the people of God 'in Christ'. The emphasis, not only in the Gospels but everywhere, is upon the person and the work of Christ. This gives the New Testament a marked unity and concentration, over-riding all the diversities of its writings. It is not only concerned with a single, brief, momentous episode in history, but it is entirely dominated by a single Personality.

The books of the New Testament were written in response to the changing needs of a swiftly moving situation. Some of them are strictly 'occasional' writings, called forth by some passing emergency. All of them are marked more or less by the idiosyncrasies of author, place and time. Analytical criticism has emphasized their differences, and in doing so has often brought into clearer relief this or that element in the thought and life of early Christianity. But to read the documents again, after analysis has done its work, is to be convinced that all these writers not only share a common fundamental outlook, and a common interest in certain broad themes, but also work upon a certain accepted pattern of thought, which shows up, sometimes in direct statement, sometimes allusively, through all the specialized forms of composition, whether story or homily, argument, prophecy or hymn.

This pattern was in fact embodied in what the early Christians called 'the Proclamation'. The word in our versions is 'the Preaching'; but an experience of modern preaching might perhaps suggest something different from what the word implied. The Greek word is *kerygma*. The verb *keryssein* means to announce or proclaim. A *keryx* was a town-crier, an auctioneer or a herald (an 'announcer', shall we say?). The *kerygma* is what he announces or proclaims. The first exponents of Christianity regarded themselves as 'heralds' or 'announcers', with a 'proclamation' to publish abroad.[1] Such a proclamation has (as we say) 'news-value'. In fact, when they were thinking of its content rather than its form, they spoke of it as 'the Good News' (in our translation, 'Gospel').

The general form and content of the 'Proclamation' can be discovered from the account given in the Acts of the Apostles of the preaching of Peter and Paul,[2] considered along with other writings, and it can be dated with the help of the Pauline Epistles to the earliest period of the Church. It was not rigidly stereotyped; it had no fixed verbal form; but with some freedom of variation in details it preserved a common and generally recognized pattern. Its scheme was as follows.[3]

1. *Fulfilment*

The Proclamation opens with an announcement that the long-expected climax of the history of God's people has

---

1 The correct translation of these terms is given in the margin of the R.V. of the Pastoral Epistles, I Timothy ii. 7; II Timothy i. 11, iv. 17; Titus i. 3.

2 See Acts ii. 14–39, iii. 13–26, iv. 10–20, v. 30–32, x. 36–43, xiii. 17–41.

3 For a fuller discussion I may refer to my book *The Apostolic Preaching and its Developments*.

arrived. His purpose in it all, disclosed by the prophets, is now fulfilled. This theme is elaborated by references to various passages in the Old Testament. Such passages are freely quoted in almost every part of the New Testament. Usually it will pay the student to look up such passages in their Old Testament context, for they will be found often to throw unexpected light upon the meaning of New Testament ideas. But apart from any particular applications of prophecy, we are to understand that everything else that the Proclamation contains is governed by this maxim: 'The time is fulfilled, and the Kingdom of God is at hand'.[1] In these terms Mark has summarized the first utterances of Jesus in Galilee. They govern equally the proclamation of His apostles.

2. *The Story*

The fulfilment took the form of a series of events, which are recounted as they were handed down by the first witnesses. The way in which this was done we may gather from such an example as the speech put into the mouth of Peter at his interview with the friendly Roman officer Cornelius of Caesarea. With almost telegraphic brevity it reviews the salient facts of the story of Jesus:

You know the thing that happened throughout all Judaea, beginning from Galilee, after the Baptism that John proclaimed: Jesus of Nazareth—how God anointed him with holy Spirit and power: who went about doing good, and healing all who were oppressed by the devil, because God was with him; and we ourselves are witnesses of all that he did in the country of the Jews and in Jerusalem; whom they killed by hanging on a tree. This person God raised up on the third day, and permitted him to be visible, not to the whole people, but to witnesses chosen in advance by God— namely to us, who ate and drank with him after his resurrec-

1 Mark i. 14–15.

tion from the dead. And he enjoined us to proclaim to the people and to affirm that this is he who is appointed by God judge of living and dead.[1]

This looks like notes for a speech rather than the speech itself: a kind of outline for preachers. It appears that Paul is quoting from the closing paragraphs of some similar *précis* in writing to the Corinthian church about A.D. 54:

I handed on to you what I had received: that Christ died for our sins according to the Scriptures; that he was buried; and that he was raised on the third day according to the Scriptures, and appeared to Cephas [Peter] and then to the Twelve....So whether it is I or they, this is what we proclaim, and this is what you believed.[2]

These bald summaries, in which we recognize already the outlines of the narratives in the Gospels, could no doubt be filled in with detail according to the speaker's ability and the demands of the occasion; but it was essential to the Proclamation that the plain facts of the case should be communicated, because it was these that constituted the fulfilment of God's purpose in history. We shall return to the story presently. Meanwhile we pass on to the next section of the Proclamation.

3. *The Consequences*

The outcome of the events narrated was the emergence of the Church itself as the new 'Israel of God'. It was marked as such by the gift of the Spirit. The prophets, we may recall, had spoken of the Spirit of God as the power which would give new life to His people in the age to come.[3] The early Christians affirmed that this had come true. They were conscious of living in the presence and power of the living God; in immediate contact with deep and permanent springs of life in the unseen world. In so far as that was

1 Acts x. 36–42.   2 I Corinthians xv. 1–11.
3 Especially Ezekiel xxxvi. 24–28, xxxvii. 12–14. See p. 48.

pure inwardness of spiritual experience, it does not abide our question, or our analysis. But in making the gift of the Spirit a part of their public proclamation, the early Christians did not intend to rest their case upon essentially incommunicable inward experience. They meant to say that here was a new kind of community life, exhibiting the marks of inward spiritual power in its freedom, unity, and constructive energy. In view of the actual achievements of the Church in its early days, these marks could not be denied.

The Church also appealed to 'signs and wonders', or in other words, 'miracles', as proof of the power of the Spirit. In these days we are embarrassed by alleged miracles: but they are on the record, and we must take account of them. 'I will not venture to speak', writes Paul, 'of anything but what Christ accomplished through me to bring the Gentiles into obedience, in word and deed, in the power of signs and wonders, in the power of Holy Spirit.'[1] Again, in a catalogue of 'gifts of the Spirit', he includes 'works of power, gifts of healing, [unusual] kinds of speech',[2] as if they were everyday phenomena of Church life. That is first-hand evidence that extraordinary things did happen, which were taken, *bona fide*, to be 'miraculous'. We may think that if we had been there, with our present knowledge, we could have explained them by 'natural' causes (such as 'autosuggestion', 'telepathy', 'extrasensory perception'—if indeed such terms do explain anything). But it remains that we were not there and Paul was.

It is however significant that in the passage just quoted his point is that while these 'works of power' no doubt have their value, they are far from being the most important or essential marks of life in the Spirit. More important are the gifts of wisdom and knowledge which the Church possesses 'by the same Spirit'[3] (and we have already noticed the

1 Romans xv. 18–19.   2 I Corinthians xii. 28.
3 I Corinthians xii. 8–11.

astonishing intellectual achievements of the first two generations of Christian thinkers). Most important of all is the gift
of 'charity' or 'love',[1] in the sense of an outgoing energy of
goodwill towards all men (not affectionate sentiments), expressed in definite ways of action, within the community and
in its external relations.

In 'proclaiming' the Spirit, therefore, the Church was
speaking of overt facts, and referring them to their unseen
cause, the immanence, or 'indwelling', of the Spirit of God.
For the first Christians never supposed that they would ever
have been competent, of themselves, to bring such a community into being. It was the work of God, through Christ.
As the 'outpouring' of the Spirit had come, unsought, in
consequence of the life, death and resurrection of Christ, so
the 'indwelling' of the Spirit was the means by which He
continued to form, guide and govern His Church out of the
unseen world, where He was now invested with divine
authority 'at the right hand of God'.

Christ in heaven: His Spirit dwelling in the Church on
earth: that meant that there was continuous 'two-way
traffic' between the seen and the unseen. The powers of the
eternal world invaded the world of time, and human life was
transfigured with the glory of the unseen. This sense of the
immediate imminence of the eternal order, and of Christ's
supreme authority exerted out of the unseen world, took form
in the belief that at any moment He might 'come again in
glory' and bring history to an end. The first generation, or
many of them, expected that this would happen well within
their lifetime. It did not happen. The faith of the Church
adapted itself to the disappointment of its first expectations
with little disturbance, beyond a deepening of the conviction
that through the Spirit Christ had already 'come again' to
His people,[2] to reign over them for ever 'until the consum-

1 I Corinthians xii. 31–xiii. 3.   2 John xiv. 16–23.

mation of the Age'.[1] Meanwhile, 'to depart and be with Christ'[2] was the natural sequel to a life 'in Christ' here and now.

4. *The Appeal*

Finally, the Proclamation led up to an appeal to the hearers to give their personal assent to the 'Good News'; to implement it by turning in repentance and trust to God, who by His 'mighty works' had made a new people for Himself; and to signify the same by baptism into the fellowship of the Church, thereby accepting God's forgiveness and entering into new relations with Him.

In this 'proclamation', then, we have the shape into which the formative convictions of Christianity were cast by its first exponents. It underlies every part of the New Testament. But there was something more to be said. The proclamation set forth an act of God by which He established a 'new covenant'. A covenant necessarily involves obligation. In the Old Testament, after God had 'redeemed' His people by His 'mighty acts' at the Red Sea, He bound them by covenant to obey His Law, which was given at Sinai. And so, in the New Testament, the 'new covenant' set up through the work of Christ, carries with it a 'new commandment'.[3]

There is a Christian Law[4] as well as a Christian Gospel. But the New Testament has a fresh understanding of the nature of law. The Jewish 'law of commandments contained in ordinances'[5] (as Paul defines it, with his accustomed precision) is abolished. It was bound up with local, national, and essentially temporary conditions which a universal religion must shed.

Those followers of the prophets, however, who had col-

1 Matthew xxviii. 20. 2 Philippians i. 23.
3 John xiii. 34; I John ii. 7–11. 4 Galatians vi. 2.
5 Ephesians ii. 15.

lected, codified and developed the so-called 'laws of Moses'
believed that in them they possessed the clue to something
deeper and more permanent: the eternal Moral Law itself;
the pattern of God's will for His creatures. Moreover, they
were quite aware that *this* 'law' was not confined to 'commandments contained in ordinances'. Indeed our word 'law'
is not an adequate equivalent for the Hebrew term, *Torah*,
which it represents in our versions. (Translation is an art
in which complete success is impossible, since it is rarely
that corresponding words in different languages cover precisely the same range of meanings.) *Torah* means, by its
etymology, something like 'teaching' or 'instruction'. In Old
Testament usage it means instruction in the ways of God and
His demands upon men, whether given by means of positive
precepts and statutes, or by other means. Although the Five
Books of Moses, containing the codes of Hebrew Law, are
specifically called the *Torah*, the prophets often speak of their
own teaching (delivered not as their own, but as the 'word
of the Lord') as *Torah*, though it never had statutory force.
It was an exposition of the ways of God with men, carrying
implications about His demands upon them.

Thus the term 'law', in the New Testament as well as
in the Old, is capable of a range of meaning wider than
properly belongs to the English word. We might define it as
an interpretation of the character of God and His relations
with men, in terms of His moral demands. Hence the Law
of Christ is fundamentally an interpretation, in terms of
ethical obligation, of the character of God as disclosed in the
person and work of Christ. This is often indicated in the
actual form of the precepts given in Gospels and Epistles
alike. 'Love your enemies...that ye may be sons of your
Father in heaven.'[1] 'Be ye merciful, as your Father is
merciful.'[2] 'Be ye kind one to another, tender-hearted, for-

1 Matthew v. 44–45.　　　　2 Luke vi. 36.

giving one another, even as God also in Christ forgave you.'[1] Such precepts clearly depend for their full meaning upon the 'proclamation' of what God has done for men through Christ.

Since the work of Christ can be comprehensively described as the expression of the divine charity, or love, towards men, the whole of the Moral Law can accordingly be summed up in the 'new commandment'—'love one another as I have loved you'.[2] But the truth can equally well be expressed without using imperatives at all. 'God is love; and he that dwelleth in love dwelleth in God, and God in him.... We love, because He first loved us.'[3] This may be said to be the final statement of the Law of Christ, though it is in entirely non-legal terms.

It would however be misleading to suggest that the ethical teaching of the New Testament is sufficiently represented by some such very general proposition (as if it were enough to say 'Love, and do as you like'). In Gospels and Epistles alike we have a considerable body of explicit directions for Christian conduct. If we consider (say) the Sermon on the Mount, or such examples of apostolic ethics as Romans xii–xiv, or Ephesians iv–vi, we recognize a distinctive method of moral instruction, which differs from contemporary models, whether Jewish or Greek. We are not given a series of deductions from a general rule (like—shall we say?—Aristotle's rule that virtue lies in the mean, a maxim which he shows, over the space of several books, to be exemplified in the virtues of courage, temperance, justice, and the rest). Nor, on the other hand, are we given a code of precise rules of observance, adapted, so far as possible, to cover all contingencies (which was the aim of Jewish Rabbinical teaching). We are given a survey of a large variety of typical concrete situations in which people find themselves, and these situations are set in the light of what God has done for men in Christ.

1 Ephesians iv. 32.   2 John xiii. 34.   3 I John iv. 16, 19.

Thus, in the Sermon on the Mount we are introduced to the problems (among others) of quarrels and law-suits, marriage-relationships, political oppression, the accumulation of wealth and the insecurity of the poor. In Romans xii–xiv we have in part a different set of problems, which arose as the Church grew and spread abroad in a pagan society: such as those of individual and social distinctions within the community, relations with friendly and with hostile pagans, the State and its demands, and so forth. In Ephesians iv–vi we have in addition the specific problems of family life and of the relations of masters and slaves. With all brevity, the situations are presented in a concrete and realistic way. But observe the setting.

In the Epistle to the Romans, Paul has spent eight chapters in an elaborate exposition of the 'Gospel of God', an exposition enriched with considerable learning and with a penetrating psychological insight, but always based directly upon the 'Proclamation'. Next, in chapters ix–xi he places the Gospel in the context of a philosophy of history and relates it to a doctrine of divine providence. Then and not till then, at the beginning of Chapter xii, he opens up the theme of Christian ethics, in the words, 'I beseech you therefore, brethren, by the mercies of God...'. In the word 'therefore' lies much virtue: it implies that the direction of Christian action, in the variety of situations to be reviewed, is always to be determined by reference to what God has done for us in Christ.

There is a most striking example of this in Chapter xiv, which discusses in detail a situation where sincere Christians then differed conscientiously upon matters of conduct (Sabbath-keeping and vegetarianism). We know only too well the devastating results which can follow from an intolerant insistence upon conscientious convictions. We know also that at times it has been only through a relentless insistence upon such convictions *contra mundum* that the truth has been saved. There is a perennial problem. Paul does not provide any cut-and-dried solution. He insists that the problem shall be considered in the light of these two principles, derived from the Gospel itself: 'No one of us lives to himself, and no one dies to himself.... Whether we live or die, we belong to the Lord; indeed it was for this that Christ died and rose again, to become Lord of living and dead'; and, 'You must not ruin...him for whom Christ died'.

In the Epistle to the Ephesians, again, we have first, in chapters i–iii, a long passage which deals, by way of contemplation rather than argument or exposition, with the great themes of the Gospel, and then, in logical dependence upon it, a passage of ethical instruction, beginning at iv. 1.

Here we may take as an outstanding example of method, the treatment of marriage.[1] 'Husbands, love your wives as Christ loved the Church and gave Himself up for it.' From this starting-point an entirely new conception of married love is developed, arising directly out of a consideration of what Christ did for us. It is here, and not in any abstract principle, that the Christian doctrine of marriage has its roots.

The Sermon on the Mount, similarly, begins with the Beatitudes, which proclaim the blessings inherent in the Kingdom of God. As we have seen, one way of putting the results of the coming of Christ, and particularly of His death and resurrection, is to say that the Kingdom of God, with all its benefits, has thereby become accessible to men. Thus the precepts of the Sermon on the Mount are addressed to those who have 'received the Kingdom of God', or, in other words, have entered into the New Covenant. Indeed, we might say that every such precept depends upon a major premiss—'The Kingdom of God has come upon you'.[2] Since this is so— 'Love your enemies, that you may be sons of your Father

1 Ephesians v. 25–33.   2 Matthew xii. 28; Luke x. 9.

in heaven'[1] (sonship in God's family being an aspect of the New Covenant). Since this is so—'Be not anxious for the morrow...but seek first His Kingdom and righteousness'.[2] 'Judge not, that ye be not judged'[3]—since the Kingdom of God, with all its blessings, comes also as judgement.

Among the precepts of Christ in the Gospels, and the precepts with which they are illustrated and supplemented in the Epistles, there are few which could be applied as positive rules, to be followed mechanically, and enforced if necessary by legal sanctions. They indicate the *direction* which Christian action must take, and the *standard* by which it must be judged. The Gospel precepts, on the whole, differ from those in the Epistles in making no attempt to accommodate Christian obligation to the practical possibilities of the human situation. They represent the 'absolute ethics' of the Kingdom of God, which is 'not of this world', though it comes in this world. We are not to suppose that we are capable in this world of loving our enemies (or even our neighbours), to the full measure in which God has loved us; or of being as completely disinterested and single-minded, as pure of worldly desire and anxiety, and as unreserved in self-sacrifice, as the words of Jesus demand; and yet these are the standards by which all our actions are judged. The obligations, in fact, which the New Covenant lays upon us can never be exhausted: man's reach must always exceed his grasp. 'When you have done all, say, "We are unprofitable servants; we have only done our duty".'[4]

Thus the Law of Christ serves to keep conscience awake and to nerve the will for effort and conflict. Its effect upon one who takes it seriously is well expressed by Paul, in a passage where he has defined the meaning of the Christian life precisely in terms of the Gospel, as sharing Christ's-

1 Matthew v. 44–45. 2 Matthew vi. 25–33.
3 Matthew vii. 1. 4 Luke xvii. 10.

sufferings, being conformed to His death, and experiencing the power of His resurrection. He goes on:

I do not consider that I have yet attained; but one thing I do: forgetting what lies behind and stretching out to what lies before, I press on towards the goal, for the prize of God's upward calling in Christ Jesus.[1]

Such is the Law of Christ, as it was conceived by the writers of the New Testament: an interpretation, in terms of ethical obligation, of God's ways with men in Christ. The authoritative basis of interpretation was found in the teaching of Jesus Himself. He left nothing in writing; but His sayings, like those of Jewish Rabbis of the time, were remembered and transmitted by word of mouth by His disciples. Later, as the Church grew, the work of instructing converts in the Christian 'way' (as it was called) was entrusted to an accredited order of 'teachers'. For the purposes of this 'catechetical instruction' collections of Sayings of the Lord were compiled, in which His words were translated out of their original Aramaic into Greek, and arranged, sometimes with explanatory additions, to meet the changing needs of different communities.

Written compilations began, probably, almost as soon as the Church moved into Greek-speaking regions.[2] They continued to be made until well on in the second century, upon

1 Philippians iii. 8–14.

2 It is a moot point whether Paul cites the Sayings from a written source or after oral tradition. That he and his converts knew an authoritative body of such sayings is certain. The way in which he makes use of it is illuminating. Writing to the Church at Corinth, about A.D. 54, upon some disputed points of Christian behaviour, he settles the question by quoting an 'injunction of the Lord', where tradition attests such an injunction. In other cases he has to be content with giving his own 'opinion', guided, as he believes, by the Spirit. It was thus that the system of Christian ethics grew up. (See I Corinthians vii. 10–13, 25.)

the basis of still floating oral tradition. Some of the oldest and best authenticated collections of Sayings of the Lord were used in the composition of the Gospels, particularly the first and third, which taken together give a fairly full conspectus of the teaching of Jesus Christ. Other New Testament writings, however, also presuppose an extensive acquaintance with the Sayings, though they are not usually quoted in express terms, but referred to allusively. A close verbal study of such writings as the Epistle of James, the First Epistle of John, and the ethical sections of most of the Pauline Epistles, is needed to show how deeply embedded in the teaching of the early Church was the tradition of the words of Jesus which gave authority to it all.

Here then are the essential ingredients of the religion of the New Testament: the Gospel of Christ and the Law of Christ. Both are assumed as fundamental in Gospels and Epistles alike. Both, obviously, have meaning only as they are referred to the historical personality, and the work, of Jesus Christ. The Gospel has its centre in the story of Jesus; the Law derives its authority from His teaching. It remains to review briefly the historical episode of which He was the centre, and to try to understand its place in the process of history which we have been following.

We have seen that the prophets recognized a pattern in the history of their people, which betrayed its divine meaning. History, they said, means God confronting man in judgement and mercy, and challenging him with a call, to which he must respond. This pattern recurs in the story of the Gospels.

The Jewish people were once more under foreign domination. Rome had appeared in Palestine, first as an 'ally' of Jewish princes, then as a 'protecting power'. Finally, Judaea was reduced to the position of a province governed by an imperial official, while the rest of the country was left to native princes responsible to the emperor.

A certain number of Jews, principally those of aristocratic priestly families, accepted the situation, and tried, by a cautious subservience to the conquerors, to preserve such partial autonomy as Rome allowed, under their own leadership. The substance of their power consisted in tenure of the high priest-hood and control of the Temple. (They are the 'chief priests' and 'Sadducees' of the Gospels.)

At the other extreme stood a body of patriotic malcontents. While Jesus was a boy, they had risen in revolt under one Judas the Gaulonite. The revolt was put down with ruthless thoroughness: hundreds were crucified. But from then on an 'underground front' (the 'Zealots', as they liked to be called) kept the government on tenterhooks.

Meanwhile the most respected religious leaders (the 'scribes and Pharisees' of the Gospels) advocated a policy of passive submission, combined with an ever-tightening internal disci-pline, until it should please God to intervene and 'set up His Kingdom', as the prophets had foretold. The discipline by which the nation was to be consolidated was based upon a scrupulous observance of the Law of Moses, as expounded and amplified by the 'scribes'.

Popular piety and patriotism at once were fed upon 'apocalypses' which depicted the approaching downfall of the enemies of Israel and the aggrandisement of the chosen people. Some of them combined such hopes with visions of the End of the World. Others kept nearer to the level of common experience, forecasting a great victory granted miraculously to a divinely appointed leader, the 'Messiah', who should then reign in righteousness over an Israelite empire. How far these fantastic visions of the future were countenanced by the leaders of religious thought we cannot say with certainty. What is certain is that 'Messianic' expectations kept the minds of the people in a ferment. The scribes might counsel a humble waiting for God's appointed time, but for the 'man in the street' that meant no more than postponing for a while the fulfilment of the same national ambitions, and the satisfying of the same national grudges, which the Zealots proposed to settle out of hand by 'direct action'.

It was a situation of almost intolerable tension. Political and religious animosities distracted the country. Roman governors tried in turn conciliation and intimidation, but it made little difference. Hatred of the 'heathen' embittered the whole of Jewish life, while fear of their power bred an increasing sense of frustration. There could be only one issue, failing some far-reaching change of heart. As Jeremiah saw with a tragic inevitableness the approach of the Babylonian conquest, so Jesus saw divine judgement impending over His people by the sword of Rome: 'Except ye repent, ye shall all in like manner perish!'.[1] The warning passed unheeded. A generation later the unceasing feuds within the nation led directly to a hopeless rebellion and its foredoomed result. Jerusalem was destroyed, never to rise again, to this day, as a Jewish city. The Jewish state disappeared from history.

Such is the background of the Gospel story. We must recognize that behind these sordid struggles there lay a real conflict of ideals. Rome may have laid a heavy hand upon turbulent peoples, but the Roman peace was a boon to a large part of the human race. Yet Jewish thinkers were right in believing that they possessed in their own national tradition something of higher value than a secular civilization could offer. The Zealots, fanatical as they were, had no ignoble

[1] Luke xiii. 1–5. 'In like manner', i.e. as the context shows, you will be overwhelmed in the ruins of Jerusalem and perish by the sword of Rome.

cause to fight for, and they gave an example of uncalculating courage in a not very heroic age. The narrowness and rigidity of the Pharisees were designed to safeguard, in circumstances of extreme difficulty, an area within which a high religion might be practised in its purity. Even the worldly Sadducees might have put up a plausible case for their policy of 'appeasement'. Yet the total situation was pregnant with disaster.

Into this situation Jesus entered. Nothing is clearer in the Gospel story than His increasing isolation among the contending forces. It was not that He courted hostility. He had friendly relations with individuals in all the rival groups. He mixed socially both with devout Pharisees[1] and with the 'publicans'[2] who collected taxes for the hated foreign government. He recruited one of His twelve assistants from the Zealot party.[3] One of His most loyal friends belonged to the circle of the High Priest.[4] He was glad to make the acquaintance of a Roman officer who approached Him, and He expressed admiration for his simple soldierly outlook.[5] His favourite associates, it is true, were found among those who were for one reason or another treated as 'outsiders',[6] and this in itself made Him suspect to the stricter sort of Pharisee. He offended them even more deeply by His criticism of their elaborate use of religious observance. They insisted upon it as an indivisible whole; He distinguished between essentials and non-essentials, singling out, in words which pointedly recalled a famous prophecy of the Old Testament, 'justice,

1 Luke vii. 36, xiv. 1.
2 Mark ii. 14–17; Luke xix. 1–10.
3 Luke vi. 15. (Matthew x. 4 and Mark iii. 18 give the Aramaic equivalent 'Cananaean' (not 'Canaanite').)
4 John xviii. 15: the Greek implies something more definite than mere 'acquaintance'.
5 Matthew viii. 5–13; Luke vii. 1–10.
6 Matthew xi. 19; Luke xv. 1–2.

mercy and faith' as the 'weightier matters of the Law'.[1]
The moral authority which He assumed was resisted by the
official 'scribes'.[2] He offended the priestly aristocracy beyond
pardon by actively interfering with the use of the Temple
courts as a public market and exchange, which brought them
in a handsome revenue.[3] The patriotic party He alienated by
refusing to deny the emperor's claim to tribute from the
conquered[4]—the very point on which the revolt of Judas the
Gaulonite had turned. At the same time He made it easy
for His enemies to denounce Him to the Roman government
when He allowed the populace to acclaim Him as a deliverer.[5]
Thus it came about that all the rival parties agreed for a
moment to hunt Him to death, before turning again to their
unending quarrels.

It would however be a mistake to conclude that these
almost incidental collisions are sufficient to account for the
isolation of Jesus. In contrast to the relative and partial ideals
for which the various groups contended, He stood for something absolute: the Kingdom of God. Many of those who
heard Him speak of it were accustomed to think of the
Kingdom of God as that which would come at long last,
when all the highest human hopes would reach fulfilment,
and God's purpose for man would be achieved. This desired
consummation they conceived more or less crudely, more or
less vaguely, more or less worthily, according to differences
of mind, temperament and training. At its highest it meant
this at any rate: God at last revealed to men in His power
and glory, shaping human life to His will, and transfiguring
it in the light of His presence. For the rest—'Eye hath not

1 Matthew xxiii. 23; cf. Micah vi. 8.
2 Mark i. 21–22, ii. 7, ii. 23–iii. 6.
3 Mark xi. 15–19, 27–33.
4 Mark xii. 13–17.
5 Mark xi. 8–10; cf. Luke xxiii. 2.

seen, nor ear heard, neither hath it entered into the heart of man'.[1]

Jesus said, 'The Kingdom of God is at hand'; 'The Kingdom of God has come upon you'[2]—it is here!

Blessed are the eyes that see what you see! I tell you, many prophets and kings desired to see what you see, and never saw it; to hear what you hear, and never heard it.[3]

There was no evidence of its coming, of the kind that people had imagined; no vast revolution in human affairs, no cataclysm, not even a sudden and far-reaching moral reformation. Admittedly the coming of the Kingdom of God was a 'mystery'.[4] Jesus could only tell them what it was 'like', using the most homely illustrations. It was like hidden treasure,[5] like corn that grows to ripeness 'man knows not how',[6] like a feast,[7] like catching fish,[8] like leaven working in dough,[9] like an employer paying wages at the end of the day.[10] The illustrations are designed to provoke thought rather than to close the question. But it is clear that they have one common point of reference. In one way or another they refer to what Jesus was doing, and to the effect of what He was doing upon the total scene. It was in Jesus Himself and in His impact upon the situation that the Kingdom of God came upon men; that God was revealed in His power and glory, to shape human life to His will. It is this that

---

1 I Corinthians ii. 9: Paul quotes the passage, as we are credibly informed by ancient scholars, from a Jewish apocalypse which has since been lost.

2 Mark i. 15; Luke x. 9, 11; Matthew xii. 28.

3 Luke x. 23–24. 4 Mark iv. 11.

5 Matthew xiii. 44. 6 Mark iv. 26–29.

7 Matthew xxii. 2–10. 8 Matthew xiii. 47–48.

9 Matthew xiii. 33.

10 Matthew xx. 1–15. For a discussion of the meaning and application of these parables I may refer to my book *The Parables of the Kingdom*.

the Gospels are telling us when they draw attention to the 'authority' with which Jesus took command of men and their destiny, and to the immense power of His 'compassion' to heal and renew.

It is this, also, that they are telling us when they relate 'miracles' that He performed. In the Fourth Gospel we are taught to think of these less as prodigies than as 'signs', that is to say, symbolic actions, having a meaning deeper than their ostensible effects. For example, the Feeding of the Multitude is to be understood not simply as a matter of staying the hunger of a large crowd on an inadequate supply of 'loaves and fishes', but as signifying the satisfaction of spiritual need with the 'bread of life'.[1]

With this clue we can see that, whatever we may make of particular 'miracles', the miracle-stories as a whole are saying precisely this: that where Jesus was, there was some incalculable and unaccountable energy at work for the dispersal of evil forces and the total renewal of human life; and that this was nothing less than the creative energy of the living God. 'Incalculable and unaccountable', I say, for the narratives constantly betray a baffled wonderment; but not magical or irrational, because they are congruous with the account which Jesus gave of the character of God: the 'Father in heaven', who is 'good' with a goodness beyond justice,[2] supported by sufficient power;[3] and who persistently takes the initiative in giving good gifts to His creatures.[4] This account He made credible through the effect of what He was and what He did.

Thus the Kingdom of God is no longer a visionary ideal, or a remote goal of the historical process. It has broken into

---

1 John vi. 26–27. Cf. the symbolic actions of the prophets, p. 17.
2 Mark x. 18; Matthew v. 45; Luke vi. 35; Matthew xx. 1–15.
3 Mark x. 27, xiv. 36.   4 Matthew vi. 25–33.

history to establish a living centre of creative energy, embodied in the action of Jesus Himself; energy that makes a decisive impact upon those who come within His orbit, and transforms events and situations, because it is the power of the living God. Here indeed was God confronting men with His call.

The response to it was at the outset mainly negative. Jesus met with opposition everywhere, because the evil inherent in the situation reacted against the presence of a goodness beyond human measures. The specious virtue, which, as we have seen, could rightly be claimed by all contending parties, was mixed up with the basest vices of our nature: greed, spite, envy, cowardice, treachery, brutality, and the rest. As Jesus moved through the scene, these evil things declared themselves. All through the narrative we are aware that men are coming up for judgement before Him; nowhere more clearly than in the story of His arrest, trial and execution as a criminal and a rebel. It is a masterpiece of dramatic irony; for while ostensibly Jesus is on His trial before council, king and governor, we are clearly aware that the real prisoners in the dock are Caiaphas, Herod and Pilate, the priests and the blind mob, as well as the traitor Judas and the disloyal disciples who denied and deserted their Master. This (as we read in the Fourth Gospel) is the Judgement of the World.[1]

We now turn back to the interpretation of history which we found in the prophets. They said that when the Kingdom of God comes, it comes in judgement; it must be so, in a world rebellious against His will; and judgement is marked by disaster and suffering. But here is judgement in paradoxical form; for the suffering is borne by the One who, Himself innocent, judges evil by His very goodness.

The New Testament writers offer a clue to the paradox

1 John xii. 31.

by referring us to a famous prophecy of the 'Second Isaiah'.[1]
There is every reason to believe that the reference is due to
Jesus Himself. In a series of poems the prophet described
the ideal 'Servant of God': his character, calling and work.
The last of these poems depicts his fate.

> He was despised and rejected of men;
>   A man of sorrows and acquainted with grief.
> And as one from whom men hide their face
>   He was despised and we esteemed him not. . . .
> He was oppressed, yet he humbled himself
>   And opened not his mouth;
> As a lamb that is led to the slaughter,
>   And as a sheep that before her shearers is dumb;
>   Yea, he opened not his mouth. . . .
> And they made his grave with the wicked
>   And with the rich in his death.[2]

Such is the fate that awaits, in a world like this, the true
Servant of God, who lives only to do His will. He bears in
his own body the consequences of other men's ill-doing,
which are the appointed judgement upon sin.

> Surely he hath borne *our* griefs,
>   And carried *our* sorrows. . . .
> He was wounded for *our* transgressions,
>   He was bruised for *our* iniquities.
> The chastisement of our peace was upon him,
>   And by his stripes we are healed.[3]

For suffering thus borne, willingly and without resentment,
becomes a means towards the healing of wrongs, and the
ultimate victory of good over evil.

This prophetic picture of the suffering that heals came true

[1] See pp. 49–50.
[2] Isaiah liii. 3, 7, 9; quoted Acts viii. 32–33.
[3] Isaiah liii. 4, 5.

in the sufferings of Jesus. The whole weight of the evil that was resident in the situation fell upon Him. He bore it willingly and without resentment, and by doing so set healing forces to work. Here at last the two sides of the divine action in history, which the prophets described as God's judgement and His mercy, are organically related. On the one hand, the story of the sufferings of Jesus is the story of the Judgement of the world (in the sense already explained). On the other hand, it shows us (through the way in which the sufferings were borne) what was the nature of that divine energy which worked in all His actions. It was indeed a goodness beyond justice. It was sheer goodwill towards all God's creatures, taking no account of fitness or desert, and refusing to be worn down or turned aside by any recalcitrance in its objects. In brief, it was the love of God.

Those who witnessed the crucifixion of Jesus could see no more than the miserable end of a defeated man. Indeed the picture, as framed within that moment of time, is one of sheer disaster. So it appeared to the followers of Jesus. But no moment in history stands by itself. Two days later they saw it all in a quite different perspective. The Gospels end with the resurrection of Jesus; and it needs no great penetration to see that their whole story is leading up to this conclusion, which alone gives meaning to it.[1]

To the first Christians, the resurrection of Christ meant two things principally. It meant first that the Master whom they had deserted at the crisis of His fate forgave them for their desertion and returned to give them a second chance.[2] When they lost Him, and lost Him by their own disloyalty as well as by the act of His enemies, life seemed at an end. His forgiveness was a new beginning.

[1] On the resurrection of Christ, see further, chap. v, pp. 102–104.
[2] This is especially clear in John xxi; how Jesus came back to Peter who had denied Him.

Secondly, His resurrection meant that the crucifixion could no longer be regarded as a meaningless failure. It was the appointed means towards final victory—God's victory over all the evil things. Death and resurrection: they saw that this is the pattern into which history falls, as God's purpose is realized in it. The prophets had divined the truth. It was now manifest. The pattern of history was 'fulfilled'. In judgement and mercy, through disaster and renewal, God confronted men conclusively, with a call that could not be evaded. Some few responded in faith and obedience, and the new order began.

It was thus that the Church came into existence. It started, not because the followers of Jesus, impressed by His teachings, decided to organize a society to perpetuate them, but directly as the result of the twofold event of His death and resurrection. In this event they now saw the act of God inaugurating the 'new covenant', through which His people entered into newness of life.

They recalled how at the last meal they had eaten with their Master before His crucifixion He had spoken of His approaching death. Taking a loaf, He had broken it and distributed it to them, with the strange words, 'This is my body, which is [broken] for you'; and taking a cup of wine, He had said, 'This cup is the new covenant in my blood'.[1] They now understood His meaning better, and as a standing testimony to the truth, they repeated at their meals of fellow-

1 I Corinthians xi. 23–25. Similarly Mark xiv. 22–24. Paul's account was written down at least ten years earlier than Mark's. He expressly tells us, not only that he had communicated it to the Corinthians when he visited them (50 A.D.) but also that he had received it by a tradition that went directly back to Jesus Himself. This is excellent historical evidence. I have bracketed the word 'broken' because some of the best manuscripts omit it, but it is implied in the action of breaking the bread which accompanied the words.

ship what He had said and done. 'Whenever', wrote Paul, 'ye eat this bread and drink the cup, ye proclaim the Lord's death.'[1] And so the Church does still, reviving continually the living memory of the event—a memory that runs back to the time before there were any written records of it, when men spoke of it as they had seen it. There could be no more striking witness to the historical actuality of the things with which we are dealing.

1 I Corinthians xi. 26.

CHAPTER V

HISTORY AS REVELATION

WE have now reviewed briefly the contents of the Old and New Testaments, as the record of several centuries in the history of a community. This record the Church offers as a revelation of God.[1]

We may take this to mean, in the first place, that in the changing and developing thoughts of the biblical writers about God, man and the world, we have a movement of the spirit of man towards a fuller apprehension of the truth, under the guidance of the Spirit of Truth. In the process, as we have seen, comparatively crude and inadequate ideas are gradually replaced by ideas more worthy of their objects. We may think of it as a process of education. God, who is the source of all truth, communicated to men, stage by stage, as they were able to digest it, an increasing measure of knowledge about Himself. In this sense the Bible is rightly described as containing a 'progressive revelation'.

But that is not all. The Bible is not simply an account of a development of thought. It is also a history of events, in which, and particularly in certain crucial events, we are invited to trace the manifest working of the divine providence. 'The mighty acts of the Lord'[2] is a biblical phrase which stamps the whole. The God of the Bible is a 'living God'.[3] He reveals

1 Here we resume the argument where it was left in chapter 1, and continue it in view of our survey of the biblical literature in chapters III and IV.

2 Psalm cvi. 2, etc.

3 The phrase occurs at least ten times in the Old Testament and sixteen times in the New.

Himself in the movement of events. What we are dealing with is not simply a history of revelation, but history as revelation.

The word 'history', as we commonly use it, has two distinct meanings. It means both the course of events, and a record of the course of events. This ambiguity is in the nature of the case. There was published not long ago a light-hearted historical skit entitled *1066 and All That*, which, behind its nonsense, contains more sense than might appear. It starts with a definition of history: 'History is what you can remember.' That is exactly what history is. It consists of remembered events. Not everything that occurs is an historical event, capable of entering into an historical record. The occurrence must have sufficient *interest* to give it a place in the memory of those who experienced it. Not only so; it must have sufficient *public* interest to remain imprinted on the corporate memory of a community. This corporate memory may take the form of oral tradition and legend, or of commemorative monuments in stone or the like, or, finally, of written and printed records. But no event gets into such records unless it was an interesting event; that is to say, an event which had *meaning* for some sufficient number of people. An historical event is an occurrence *plus* the meaning which it had for some portion of the human race.

It is in this sense that we speak of history in the Bible. It reports events which are historical in the fullest sense, because they are laden with meaning; and these events are narrated in such a fashion as to bring out clearly the meaning which they bear. According to the unanimous view of the biblical writers, the meaning of the events resides in a meeting of man with God. It is this which gives character to the history. By this I do not mean merely that the idea of a meeting with God colours the thought of the biblical writers about events;

7-2

but that the course of events itself was what it was because it bore this meaning for those who participated in it. As we have seen, it was because the prophets interpreted the history of their time in this sense that the history of succeeding centuries followed the course it did. And it is so all through the Old and New Testaments.[1]

This means that the biblical history is controlled by a factor which belongs to the realm beyond history. The importance of the 'natural' factors which go to make history is never ignored—factors physical, geographical, biological, economic, and so forth. In fact, among ancient literatures, the Bible is rather exceptionally informative upon many such matters. But at the crucial points it is made clear that a factor beyond the natural is impinging upon the natural factors and directing their outcome. This 'super-natural' factor cannot be explained away without re-writing the Bible and falsifying the witness of its writers. Here is the real crux of belief in the supernatural. Miracle-stories lie on the fringe. Discussion of them falls into place when we have settled accounts with this central feature of the whole record: an encounter with that which transcends the whole natural order of things: the meeting of man with God.

As we follow the biblical record, we observe that the encounter with God is apt to take place when a man finds himself involved in a situation of unusual tension in the real world. The prophet is a 'public man'. His encounter with God is not private experience withdrawn from contact with workaday things, like that of the mystics and sages of many religions. The pressure of public movements and events upon his spirit is the occasion of the encounter with God which lays its compulsion upon him, and the truth which the encounter forces upon his mind is public property.

It is true that the encounter is often described in terms of

1 See pp. 50–51.

what we call 'religious experiences', sometimes of abnormal experiences, like visions or auditions. The prophet 'sees' what is invisible to the bodily eye; 'hears' words spoken when no human speaker is present. This fact sometimes causes difficulty to readers in the modern world. It is certainly true that visions and auditions may be no more than illusions. To infer (as some have done) that *all* such experiences are illusory —that Isaiah's vision was due to hysteria, or the conversion of Paul to an attack of epilepsy—is clearly illegitimate. Most of the prophets are embarrassed by the presence of 'false prophets' whose mental processes are not distinguishable psychologically from their own; and yet they remain serenely convinced that God really has spoken to them.

The Bible indeed offers rich material to the psychologist who wishes to examine the varieties of religious experience; and it is possible to exhibit the psychological mechanism of the prophetic consciousness in a fascinating way. But when the mechanism has been exposed, nothing has yet been said about the validity of the experience, or about the truth of the interpretation of life which it conveyed. Precisely that in it which was individual and creative eludes our analysis.

Two things however it seems possible to say about the validity of the prophetic experience. First, when the prophets say, 'I saw the Lord', or 'The Lord said unto me', or 'The Spirit of the Lord came upon me', we can see that the experience to which they refer was an element in a total experience of life which was rational and coherent, forming a logical unity in itself. We can see it clearly enough in prophets such as Isaiah and Jeremiah, whose biographies are in large measure open to us. Their visions and auditions were not aberrations, unrelated to their experience of life as a whole. These were clearly the kind of men of whom it is credible that they did meet with God, whatever psychological form the meeting may have taken.

Secondly, the personal experience of the prophets is also organically related to the course of history in which they played a part. It enabled them to give an interpretation of the situation which could stand up to the facts. Not only so; the effects which flowed from their intervention in history were congruous and commensurate with its alleged origin in an encounter with God. We have seen that the impact which the prophets made upon their time brought about momentous consequences, affecting the whole subsequent history of mankind in an important way. It is therefore unlikely that the experience which impelled them to speak and act as they did was a delusion, whatever the temporary form in which it may have been embodied. The prophetic experience is, in some way, of the same stuff as history itself.

I should apply this not only to the prophetic experiences of the Old Testament, but also to the somewhat similar experiences which determine the New Testament interpretation of events: I mean the appearances of the risen Christ to His followers. Here we have one strictly first-hand witness. Paul is the one New Testament writer who, speaking in his own person, expressly claims to have had an encounter with Christ after His resurrection. He goes bail for a large number of other witnesses, whose testimony is in some cases indirectly reported in the Gospels and the Acts, and he appeals confidently to their unanimity.[1] When therefore he speaks of his meeting with Christ, he is not speaking of some private, incommunicable experience, but of an experience which he shared with others, an experience of 'public' facts. Turning to Paul, then, for a first-hand description of what it meant to meet the risen Lord, we observe that he speaks in terms which recall the language of the prophets. If Isaiah says, 'I saw the Lord', Paul also says, 'Have not I seen the Lord?'[2]

1 I Corinthians xv. 3–11.
2 Isaiah vi. 1; I Corinthians ix. 1.

If Jeremiah says, 'The Lord appeared of old unto me', Paul says, 'He appeared unto me also'.[1] If Ezekiel says, 'The hand of the Lord God fell upon me', Paul says, 'I was arrested by Christ Jesus'.[2] Isaiah describes in strange and impressive symbolism his vision of the glory of God. Paul, more simply but not less impressively, speaks of 'the light of the knowledge of the glory of God in the face of Jesus Christ'.[3]

It seems clear that, upon one side at least, the New Testament experience of an encounter with the risen Christ was analogous to the prophetic experience. If we raise the question of its validity, the same tests may be applied. Paul's meeting with Christ is of a piece with his total experience of life. It is no aberration. We know Paul very intimately from his letters. They reveal a singularly coherent personality; and this coherence depends to a marked degree upon the reality of what we call his conversion. Paul says he was 'arrested' by Christ. Well, he was certainly arrested by something, to some purpose; and the effects of that 'arrest' in the whole of his career were congruous with their alleged cause. Moreover, the remoter effects in history—the rise of the Church, the highly original character of its community-life, its astonishing early expansion and its no less astonishing spiritual and intellectual achievement—were congruous and commensurate with that which the apostles declared to be the starting-point of it all: their meeting with the risen Christ, in whom they saw the glory of God. It is unlikely that all this was based upon a delusion.

I do not suggest that the apostolic witness to the resurrection of Christ can be entirely reduced to terms of prophetic

---

1 Jeremiah xxxi. 3; I Corinthians xv. 8. (In Greek the verb is identical.)

2 Ezekiel viii. 1; Philippians iii. 12.

3 II Corinthians iv. 6.

experience. Clearly there are fresh and unprecedented elements in it. To see the glory of God, as Isaiah saw it, in visionary symbols of a smoking altar served by winged seraphim, is not the same thing as for Paul to see 'the glory of God in the face of Jesus Christ', who was a known character in history, recently put to death. But it is in the features which the apostolic witness shares with the prophetic witness that we can best assess its weight.

The corroborative evidence which is adduced in the Gospels to show that the tomb where Jesus was buried was untenanted on Easter Day is secondary. It is indeed more serious and impressive than is sometimes allowed for in modern discussions. But in itself it could not be conclusive. On the one hand, if you could prove up to the hilt that the tomb was empty, you would still be far from establishing the apostolic faith that Christ was 'raised at the right hand of God'; and if, on the other hand, it could be disproved, that faith would not be refuted, since it rests upon more immediate *data*.

At its centre, the apostolic witness speaks of an encounter with God in Christ, which was like the prophetic encounter with God at least in this: that it provided a satisfying interpretation of historical events (the events of the life of Jesus as part of the history of Israel), and that it set in motion new and powerful historical forces. In assessing its weight, we are concerned with the question of the validity of religious experience and its organic relation to the actuality of history.

In both Testaments, then, everything turns upon an encounter of man with God. In reference to this encounter the biblical writers employ a characteristic formula: 'the Word of God'. The expression is obviously a metaphor; for a word, properly speaking, is the product of certain physiological processes which we cannot attribute to the Eternal. But it is a singularly appropriate metaphor, and could hardly be replaced. By means of words, and normally by no other means, one person can affect another without infringing his personal independence. I can affect another person by various kinds of direct action, to the point of compulsion; but in doing so I trespass to that extent upon his prerogative as a person (it may or may not be right or necessary at times to do so: that we need not discuss). If however I speak to him, and he hears, then of necessity he makes some kind of response— even if it be the negative response of pointedly ignoring me. The particular response is for him to determine. In any case he is affected by that which I have spoken and he has heard, while his freedom of choice remains intact. A conversation between two persons is an event in the lives of both, and in certain circumstances may be an event from which incalculable consequences flow in the world of actual, concrete facts. The word has proved a creative factor in history, on however small a scale.

Something of this kind is suggested by the biblical expression, 'the Word of God'. God makes an approach to man in a way that commands his attention and elicits a response of some kind, positive or negative. The response is not forced. Man remains free. But in proportion as he responds the Word proves a creative factor in history. As we have seen, the approach of God to men usually takes place at the point where they are keenly aware of the world-situation in which they are living. The Word of God comes, characteristically, as an interpretation of the situation, carrying with it an obligation to act. The 'inspiration' of the prophets is essentially a power of insight into the situation as expressing a meaning which is God's meaning for His people.

The Word of God, then, is the supra-historical factor which we have noted as entering into the course of history and directing it. It came to Abraham, to Moses, to prophets and apostles, not as a mere 'inner light', but as the interpretation of a situation, requiring action in that situation. Over against the evil in the situation, it came as judgement; for through the Word of God the disasters which are the necessary consequences of persistent wrong-doing are understood as His judgement upon sin. It came also, through the response of those who heard it, as a word of rescue and renewal. Thus the pattern of history as a divinely directed process was established.

The judgements and deliverances took place within the experience of a particular people: the 'chosen' people, the 'elect' of God. The idea of a chosen people has been perverted into horrible doctrines of racial and national domination, which have brought it into discredit. Yet the idea cannot be eliminated from the Bible. In recent times it has often been suggested that it may be rationalized, in the sense that the Hebrew people had a 'natural genius for religion', as the Greeks had a natural genius for philosophy, and the Romans for government—and, one might no doubt add, 'God's Englishmen' for empire-building (or is it shop-keeping?), so that we can all feel comfortable about it.

We do not however gather from the prophets the impression that they supposed their people to possess a natural genius for religion. 'Ah, sinful nation! a people laden with iniquity! a seed of evil-doers! rebellious sons!'[1] These are only a few specimens of the rich vocabulary of vituperation with which the prophets assailed their contemporaries. Nor is the case different in the New Testament. It is never suggested that the Church of God's 'elect' consists of people with a natural genius for religion. Quite the contrary. 'The Son of Man came not to call the righteous, but sinners.'[2] And there have always been Christians, and those not the worst sort, who would confess that they had a natural genius for atheism—but for the grace of God. We cannot eliminate that suggestion

1 Isaiah i. 4.
2 Mark ii. 17.

(106)

of a free act of God which is inherent in the idea of 'choice'.

God's choice, however, is (as the prophets are at pains to point out) not an act of favouritism, conferring privileges arbitrarily denied to other peoples. It is election to special responsibility.[1] To be God's chosen people means to be immediately exposed to His Word, with all the momentous consequences that flow from hearing it. That is as true of the Church in the New Testament as of Israel in the Old.[2] Of course there are privileges in hearing the Word of God, and belonging to His people; though they are hardly of such an order as to commend themselves to the *homme moyen sensuel*. But primarily, to hear the Word of God makes a man responsible before Him; and the people of God consists of those upon whom such responsibility has been laid.

We cannot pretend to explain *why* the fateful destiny of hearing the Word of God should have been laid upon this particular people. But the 'scandal of particularity', as it has been called, is inseparable from an historical revelation. History consists of events. An event happens *here* and not there, *now* and not then, to *this* person (or group) and not to that. And so the revelation of God in history came to one people and not to others, with the intention that through that people it should extend ultimately to all mankind. We cannot explain this particularity; but it is no more surprising than 'the possibility, admitted by men of science, that life has appeared only on this planet; and the certainty that only one species of terrestrial life has attained to reason, only a small minority of that species to civilization, and only a minority of that minority to a civilization progressive and scientific'.[3]

1 Amos iii. 2.

2 Cf. I Peter iv. 17: 'It is time for judgement to begin from the house of God...first from us....'

3 I quote the words of Dr Clement Webb in an article in the *Journal of Theological Studies*, vol. xliv, p. 250.

To return, then, to the main line of argument: the Bible tells how the Word of God descended upon a people, and through their varying response wrought out a course of events moving to a climax. The whole process is reviewed, briefly and conclusively, in the opening verses of the Gospel according to John, commonly called the 'Prologue' to that work.[1] It starts with the creative Word—which we have already met with in the first chapter of Genesis:[2]

> In the beginning was the Word;
>> And the Word was with God;
>> And the Word was God.
> The same was in the beginning with God.
> Through Him all things came into existence;
>> And without Him nothing came into existence.

This Word pervaded the world, as the source of life and light; but the world remained unconscious of its presence.

Then the Word, which was immanent in the entire universe, 'came' to a particular people:

> He was in the world;
> And the world was made through Him;
>> And the world did not recognize Him.
> He came to His own place,
>> And those who were His own did not receive Him.

That summarizes briefly the whole tragic history of Israel;

---

1 What follows is not intended as a complete exegesis of John i. 1–14. 'Word' is in Greek *logos*, and *logos* means also the rational principle immanent in nature and the human mind. The *logos*-doctrine of the Fourth Gospel is related to this Greek idea, but primarily its *logos* is the 'Word of the Lord' and it is on this side that it is directly related to the O.T.

2 See chap. ii, pp. 30–32.

the coming of the prophets and their rejection by a recalcitrant nation. But it was not all failure:

As many as received Him, to them He gave the right to be children of God.

These are the 'Remnant' of whom Isaiah spoke, who maintained their witness to the Word of God through national apostasy, persecution and disaster.

But even the Remnant proved inadequate to the responsibility laid upon them; the history of Israel under the Old Covenant remained inconclusive. Then there was a fresh incursion of the eternal Word into history:

> The Word became flesh,
> And dwelt among us;
> And we beheld His glory—
> Glory as of the Father's only Son—
> Full of grace and truth.

The eternal Light, which is the glory of God, is diffused through the universe ('The whole earth is full of His glory', as Isaiah heard the seraphim sing). It was revealed partially and relatively, in the religious institutions of Israel, as they increasingly conformed to the truth declared by the prophets. But now at last it was focused in the unity of a single Person, whose whole being, character and action completely embodied all that the Word of God means. It is a fresh approach of God to man; this time a final approach, conveying a decisive challenge.

The principle of 'particularity', which we have noted as inseparable from a revelation in history, has thus worked itself out to its logical conclusion. The ultimate *locus* of revelation is neither nation nor community, but a Person, who lived in Palestine and 'suffered under Pontius Pilate'. In His historic mission He gathered up the issues of a long past, and through His death and resurrection became the living centre of a new community, which has no frontiers, in time or space, short of the human race itself.

But in what sense are we to understand the life of Jesus Christ as the Word of God incarnate? We may once again approach the question from the standpoint of the prophetic interpretation of history. In history (the prophets said) the Word of God comes to men, in judgement and in renewal, calling for a response. From this point of view we may conceive the rôle of Christ in history somewhat in this way.

First, Christ uttered the Word, with final authority. His 'I say unto you' is the counterpart of the prophetic 'Thus saith the Lord'—with a significant difference. His whole teaching, as we have seen, sets up an absolute standard by which we are judged, but which also inspires a new kind of life. Not only so; His very presence among men, His attitude towards them, His action in critical human situations, constitute, no less than His sayings, a Word of God to men; for they embody concretely that which He taught about God, His character, attitude and action. 'Christ was the Word, and spake it.'

The Word of God, thus spoken, demands a response: indeed, it becomes an effective force in history only through such response. And here, secondly, Christ Himself offers, representatively, the final response. This representative character, as we have seen, is a large part of what the title 'Christ', or 'Messiah', means. When at the crisis of His fate Christ prayed, 'Not my will but thine be done',[1] He was making the response on behalf of us all, in advance, at a moment when there was no one else to make it; and making it with absolute finality.

The apostolic writers with complete unanimity lay their finger upon this one point—the *obedience* of Jesus—as the

1 Luke xxii. 42.

vital centre of all that He did for us. 'Through the obedience of the One', says Paul, 'the many will be made righteous';[1] while the Author to the Hebrews puts into the mouth of Christ the words of an ancient Psalm:[2]

> Sacrifice and offering thou didst not desire,
> But a body thou didst furnish for me.
> Holocausts and sin offerings thou didst not choose.
> Then said I, 'Behold, I come—
> In the volume of the book it is written of me—
> To do thy will, O God'.

—and then he comments, '—by which will you have been sanctified, through the offering of the body of Jesus Christ'. Here, in fact, lies the value of Christ's death: not in the physical fact of His dying, but in the perfect obedience which it expressed, releasing, as it were, the whole force of the will of God to work in history for the salvation of men.

But if the death of Christ is the seal of His perfect human obedience, it is also the climax of His revelation of the being and character of God, as absolute love. Consequently it is in the death of Christ, as the Fourth Evangelist again points out, that the glory of God is most completely revealed,[3] or in other terms, the Word is most fully made flesh.

Here, then, we have the perfect meeting of God with man, towards which the whole course of events was tending. It is at last realized in the unity of the single Personality; and henceforward this becomes the centre about which the whole movement of history turns. And thus the coming of Christ completes the biblical history, and seals its character as a course of meaningful events which are the 'mighty acts' of God, and also His 'Word' to men.

1 Romans v. 19.　　　　2 Hebrews x. 5–10.
3 John xii. 23–32.

We have now to observe that the whole story is set in a framework which is not, in the same sense, historical. It has a prologue, which is the Creation; and an epilogue, which is the Last Judgement. These first and last things can be spoken of only in symbols. They lie, obviously, outside the order of time and space to which all factual statements refer. They are not events (as the historian knows events), but realities of a supra-historical order. In referring to them the biblical writers make free use of mythology.

The distinction between history and myth is clearly marked. From Abraham to the end of the apostolic age the story is historical: it consists of actual events, directly related to the general course of history in the world. The events are sometimes seen through the medium of legend, and they may be presented in a form which leaves the actual occurrence less clear than the symbolical significance which is assigned to it.[1] But it is history, as the first and last things are not. Creation, the Fall of Man, the Deluge and the Building of Babel are symbolic myths. The Last Judgement and the End of the World, if they are not in the strict sense myths, have a similar symbolic character. The symbolism in all these cases is drawn largely from myths current among the Hebrews and other ancient peoples; but the meaning attached to the symbols—and this is the important point—is derived from the prophetic and apostolic interpretation of history. The implication is that what history had shown to be true of the dealings of God with one particular people is true of His dealings with all mankind, and indeed with the whole universe. I will now try to illustrate this in detail.

The story of the Creation in the first chapter of Genesis is, as we have already had occasion to remark, subsequent to

[1] Cf. chap. II, pp. 17–18. It is important to observe that a real event may be given symbolic value, while in other cases a myth may be created to serve as a symbol.

the work of the great prophets, and it arises out of it.[1] Its writer has projected upon the universe that which he has learned from God's dealings with Israel. He saw the state of his people as a chaos of darkness, turbulent and ungoverned. The Word of God came through Moses and the prophets, throwing light upon the darkness and creating order out of chaos. So it was, he says, in the Beginning. God spoke to primeval chaos: 'Let there be light!' He 'called the things that were not as if they were',[2] and they began to be.

This account of creation includes the statement that man was made in the image of God.[3] But that is not all there is to be said. The prophets were acutely aware that Israel, which might be expected to know and obey God as 'naturally' as migratory birds follow their annual course,[4] or a domestic animal recognizes its master,[5] did nothing of the kind. Israel's behaviour was 'unnatural', belying their origin and destiny. It must be the same (they concluded) with mankind in general. If Israel is sinful, so are other peoples; and yet they are part of God's creation, which was 'very good'. It would be 'natural' for them, in view of their origin, to obey the will of their Creator, but they do not. To express this idea, they made use of a very primitive myth (the original meaning of which may have been quite different): the story of how Adam (Hebrew for 'Man') and his wife Eve (Hebrew for 'Life') were induced by a highly mythical Serpent to disobey a command of their Maker, and in consequence were exiled from their home.[6] It is the tragic fate of Israel projected upon mankind as a whole. The Word of God that drove man out of Paradise is the word of judgement that sent Israel into exile, now given a universal application.

1 Cf. chap. ii, pp. 30–31.
2 This is Paul's striking phrase in Romans iv. 17.
3 Genesis i. 27.   4 Jeremiah viii. 7.
5 Isaiah i. 3.   6 Genesis iii.

The third of the great myths is that of the Deluge.[1] We have recently been told that archaeologists have found evidence for the Deluge as an historical event: the vast bank of mud that it deposited is still there, somewhere in Mesopotamia, 'to witness if I lie'. No doubt there was a very destructive flood in Mesopotamia in the distant past; and it is quite possible that dim memories of it coloured the Babylonian story of the adventures of Ut-napishtim, which again may have coloured the Hebrew story of the adventures of Noah. But it has very little to do with the widespread primitive myth of a supernatural deluge over the whole earth.

The biblical writer has used this old myth to set forth in symbol the idea of God's judgement coming upon man in disaster, but leading up to a new creation. For in the story Noah emerged into a world swept clean by the judgements of the Almighty, and entered into a 'covenant' with his God.

God spake unto Noah and to his sons with him, saying: 'And I, behold, I establish my covenant with you, and with your seed after you, and with every living creature that is with you, the fowl, the cattle, and every beast of the earth with you.'[2]

As Adam is all mankind, so is Noah all mankind; and the story stands as witness that God's covenant, though historically it was made with Israel, is applicable to the whole human race, and indeed to all created life—a truth finally established in the universal Gospel of the New Testament.

The story of the Building of Babel is the last of the myths of the 'first things'.[3] It is very likely that the idea of a tower whose top should reach heaven was suggested by the vast 'sky-scraper' temples whose ruins are still strewn about the lands of the Euphrates valley. It may be, as some

1 Genesis vi. 9–ix. 17.   2 Genesis ix. 9–10.
3 Genesis xi. 1–9.

have suggested, that the story of the dispersal of the builders preserves a remote memory of the break-up of some pre-historic empire. But all this concerns only the dramatic detail of the story. Essentially the story of men who defied God by trying to build up to heaven is the same as the Greek myth of the rebellious Titans who piled mountain upon mountain to storm the dwelling of the gods. Their dispersal is the judge-ment of God upon human arrogance and ambition. The story is a kind of doublet of the story of the Fall.

It serves, however, in its present setting in the Book of Genesis, to provide a background for the call of Abraham. It is out of the mass of sinful humanity, the descendants of these discomfited rebels against God, that Abraham is called. Thus the story of Babel makes a transition from the mythical to the historical. It serves to characterize mankind as lying under God's word of judgement at the moment when His creative word came to Abraham, to make a covenant and to found a people.

Thus the stories with which the Bible begins may be regarded as adaptations of primitive myths by writers who used them as symbols of truths learned in history. Nominally they refer to pre-history. In fact, they apply the principles of divine action revealed in the history of a particular people to mankind at all times and in all places. They universalize the idea of the Word of God, which is both judgement and renewal.

Much the same may be said of the conception of the Last Judgement. It is impossible to think of Doomsday as a coming event in history. An occasion which gathers together at once all the generations of men who have ever lived is obviously outside the order of space and time in which history takes place. We are dealing with symbol. The idea of the 'Day of the Lord'—God's triumph at the end of history —formed part of Israel's outlook upon the future from a very early date.[1] It underwent extensive development and elaboration in late Jewish apocalypses,[2] and their imagery is freely used by New Testament writers.

But the centre of the Christian idea of the Day of Judgement is most simply stated in Paul's words, 'We must all stand before the judgement-seat of *Christ*'.[3] We have seen that the prophetic conception of God's word of judgement in history received a profound re-interpretation in the events of the Gospel story. As Christ moved among men, displaying pure goodness in all His words and actions, men found themselves judged; and this judgement became most acute when He went to His death, because there the glory of the divine goodness was most completely disclosed. Judgement was there seen to be a by-product of actions whose aim was purely positive and creative, being the expression of the love of God. This has been put with perfect clarity in the Fourth Gospel:

God so loved the world that he gave his only-begotten son, that whosoever believeth on him should not perish, but have everlasting life. For God sent not his son into the world to condemn the world, but that the world through him might be saved.... This is the judgement: that the light is come into the world, and men loved the darkness rather than the light; for their deeds were evil.[4]

This is an interpretation of history: it tells us what happened when Jesus came among men. And this is what gives meaning to the expression 'the judgement-seat of Christ'. Behind the symbolism of Doomsday (often fantastic to our minds) this is the truth: that the verdict upon history, and upon all the actors in it, is pronounced simply by confrontation with the Word of God, made flesh in Christ. Those who had stood under His judgement in history, and acknowledged its finality, knew that He must be judge of quick and dead. As the

1 See pp. 39–40.   2 See pp. 61–64.
3 II Corinthians v. 10.   4 John iii. 16–19.

myth of the Creation and the Fall universalizes the experience of Israel in history, so the symbolism of the Last Judgement universalizes the experience of those who found themselves judged by Christ.

One thing remains. The Word of God, as we have seen, has always two aspects: it is the word of judgement, and it is the creative word of renewal. This twofold character is exemplified all through the history of the people of God, and it is taken up into the symbolic myths of the 'first things':[1] the Deluge is balanced by the covenant with Noah; the destruction of Babel provides the background for the call of Abraham. What of the 'last things'? Once again, judgement is balanced by renewal. Doomsday is followed by the 'new heavens and new earth',[2] the 'restoration of all things'.[3]

Here we are in a realm very far removed from this order of space and time. Yet even here man's experience of God's ways in history gives him some inkling of what lies beyond. When the ultimate state of mankind is symbolized by 'the holy city, New Jerusalem',[4] we have a hint that the values which long strove for expression in the little Jewish community gathered about its ancient city, are finally realized in the 'new heavens and new earth'; and when its foundation stones are said to be inscribed with the names of the twelve apostles of Christ,[5] we conclude that the foundation of the Church in history is acutely relevant to the consummation

1 The mysterious words addressed to the 'Serpent' in Genesis iii. 14–15 were taken by early Christian interpreters to imply a veiled promise of the coming of a Saviour. Then in the story of the Fall a word of renewal would balance the word of judgement. This would be in harmony with the general pattern, but there seems no suggestion of it in the actual words of Genesis, which speak only of a 'ding-dong' fight between man and the 'Serpent'.

2 II Peter iii. 13; Revelation xxi. 1.

3 Acts iii. 21.   4 Revelation xxi. 2.

5 Revelation xxi. 14.

beyond history. Little more can be said. We are in the presence of things beyond all human experience, and the Bible is notably reticent about them. One expression sums up the ultimate meaning of it all, if full weight is given to both noun and adjective: 'life eternal'. Of its character little is said, except that 'we shall be like Him, for we shall see Him as He is';[1] but this assures us once again that the life of Jesus, once lived in history, the Word made flesh, is the key to the furthest reaches of human destiny under the providence of God.

The 'prehistoric' myths, we have seen, have the effect of universalizing the meaning of the history of God's people: all mankind is comprehended in the fall of Adam; all mankind (and the lower creation) is included in the covenant with Noah. Similarly, the Last Judgement is universal. The logic of the biblical revelation seems to demand an equal universality for the final 'restoration of all things'. One New Testament writer alone explicitly draws the conclusion. Paul brings to a close his penetrating analysis of the biblical history, in Romans ix–xi, with the pregnant sentence, 'God hath shut up *all* unto disobedience, that He might have mercy upon *all*'.[2] As every human being lies under God's judgement, so every human being is ultimately destined, in His mercy, to eternal life.[3] The thought moves him to awe-struck praise of the divine Wisdom:

O the depth of the riches both of the wisdom and the knowledge of God! How unsearchable are his judgements, and his ways past finding out!...For of him, and through him, and unto him are all things. To him be glory for ever.[4]

1 I John iii. 2.   2 Romans xi. 32.
3 This 'universalism' has never been generally accepted in the Church, though it has been held by some theologians of credit in antiquity and in modern times.
4 Romans xi. 33, 36.

'Unto Him are all things.' It is not only the whole human race that enters into the new creation: for, as Paul puts it elsewhere, it is God's purpose 'to sum up all things in Christ, the things in the heavens and the things upon the earth'.[1] The entire created universe is to be 'redeemed' and 'reconciled' to its Creator,[2] 'that God may be all in all'.[3] This is the final meaning of the entire process in time.

Such is the supra-historical framework in which the historical revelation is set. Its effect is to universalize the meaning of the revelation which was given to particular people at particular times. The Word which was spoken through the prophets of Israel and made flesh in Palestine in the first century, is the same Word by which the man and his world were created, which is also the Agent of final judgement upon the quick and the dead, and the Mediator of eternal life to all men. It follows that whatever is said in Scripture about God's relations with men is not to be understood in any restrictive or exclusive sense. If the Bible records that God entered into covenant with Israel, or with the Church, by which He promised them certain blessings and laid upon them certain obligations, that is solid matter of fact, verifiable and datable in history. But it does not carry the inference that the rest of mankind is outside God's covenant, incapable of receiving His blessing, and under no obligation to Him. On the contrary, we can be sure that God speaks to all men everywhere in judgement and mercy just because He did, verifiably, so speak to His 'chosen' people in history. God's law, which in its final form is the Law of Christ, is not an optional code of behaviour for an intimate circle of peculiar people. It is the eternal moral law to which all men, as God's creatures, are responsible, and by which their actions in history are ultimately judged.

1 Ephesians i. 10. 2 Romans viii. 22–23; Colossians i. 20.
3 I Corinthians xv. 28.

We should now be in a position to set down certain very broad principles, as foundations for a religious *Weltanschauung*, or view of life, to which our study of the Bible seems to lead.

1. *God is to be met with in and through the world of things and events.* We are not called upon to deny this world, or to withdraw from its urgent realities. If we take our stand within the actual, concrete order of history to which we belong as human beings, we encounter God.

2. *God speaks to us, however, from beyond this world.* There is no question, in the Bible, of a God who is merely 'immanent' in the processes of nature with their invariable laws. Certainly, the Word of God is 'in the world' which He made. God is revealed in nature. But He transcends nature. His word 'came' to men, on occasions which can be dated and localized, and verified by their historical consequences, and each occasion is unique. The 'general revelation' of God in nature is to be understood in the light of His 'special revelation', the key to which is the 'Word made flesh' in Christ.

3. *The initiative lies with God.* Modern writers have spoken of the Bible as the record of man's search for God, and so in part it is. But the Bible itself recognizes what is at least as common a trait of human nature—man's avoidance of God. (When God walked in the garden in the cool of the day, Adam and his wife hid themselves. Their children are apt to follow their example.) What is chiefly set forth in the Bible is God's search for man. The Word of God comes often 'out of the blue', breaking in upon men's way of life. As God is not bound by the uniformities of nature, so He is not bound by conditions of preparedness in us. This is most strongly emphasized in the New Testament. It was 'while we were yet sinners' that 'Christ died for us'.

4. *The Word of God enters history both as judgement and as power of renewal.* This two-beat rhythm is characteristic. It excludes both the optimism which thinks we can 'join

the great march onward' without paying the reckoning for ancient wrongs; and the pessimism which cannot get over the *damnosa hereditas* of the irrevocable past.

5. *God calls for a response from man, which is obedience.* There can be no proper relation between the Creator and man His creature which is not a relation of sovereignty on the one part and of obedience on the other. That is why the final utterance of God's Word in Christ is described as the coming of His 'Kingdom'; and why Christ's response of perfect obedience countersigns His proclamation of the Kingdom of God, and becomes the turning-point of history.

Finally, as we survey the whole process of revelation, we are led to a conception of the life of man in this world as directed by a purpose, which is that of a Mind bent upon the creation of good; making use to that end of a wisdom of infinite subtlety and a power of unlimited resource; respecting the freedom which He has given to His creature; and using history to make Himself known to man and to win his obedience. Such is the conception of God which emerges from the biblical history as a whole. In the New Testament it is summed up, in view of the culmination of that history, in the proposition, 'God is love'; [1] with the implication that such love has at its disposal sufficient power and wisdom to attain its ends.

[1] I John iv. 8, 16.

CHAPTER VI

THE BIBLE AND THE HISTORICAL
PROBLEM OF OUR TIME

'HISTORY', said Mr Henry Ford, 'is bunk', blurting out, with a refreshing candour, what many people no doubt think. It is however a significant fact that those movements of our time which have shown the greatest power to inspire men to action on the grand scale, for good or evil, have taken the form of interpretations of history.

German National Socialism, for example, based itself on an interpretation of history through the conceptions of race and *Volkstum* ('nationality'—but the meaning of the German word is both wider and narrower). The Nazi creed is now discredited, but the wide and compelling influence which it exerted is a portent we ought not to forget—especially since there are kindred doctrines abroad in other countries which may yet raise their head. What was there in this wild and monstrous creed, which made it sweep like a prairie fire through the German people? What was there in it to impel them to action upon a scale which has proved catastrophic to the whole of Europe? There are no doubt more answers than one to that question. National Socialism was a complex phenomenon. But one side of its appeal at least could not be overlooked by anyone who happened to be in touch with Germans during the years between the Weimar revolution and Hitler's seizure of power in 1933. It offered them a task defined by an understanding of their history.

A whole generation of young Germans had emerged from

the last war humiliated, despairing and cynical. There seemed nothing to live for. Life had no meaning. Then Hitler and his followers told them that on the contrary they were living in the crucial moment of the historic destiny of the German people. The vast and turbulent centuries of European history, since the days when Arminius defeated the legions of Augustus in the Teutobürgerwald, were filled with the story of the shaping and growth of the German *Volk*; their training and discipline, through victory and disaster, to be the ultimate *Herrenvolk*. And now the moment had come. Hitler boasted that his achievement would determine the course of history for a thousand years; and they believed him. In understanding (as they thought) the meaning of their national history, and linking their own action to its agelong movement, they found their lives dignified by being absorbed in a larger purpose. They were convinced that they were making history—and they very nearly did make it to their own pattern. At least, there was here an interpretation of history which proved itself dynamic.

On the other hand, we have the Marxist interpretation of history as a 'dialectical' process, determined by economic factors; a process which takes form in our time as the final class-war between bourgeoisie and proletariate with their respective 'ideologies'. The Marxist treatment of past history is bold and imaginative, and even if it is one-sided, it brought into clear light factors which all historians now acknowledge to have been of real importance. But to the devout Marxist this interpretation of the past is no mere academic theory. It provides the one sufficient key to the understanding of the present, and assures the future; for upon Marxist premises the victory of the proletariate is a foregone conclusion. This interpretation of history has given to large numbers of people a quite new sense of meaning in their own lives, and stirred them to action under the conviction that their action is along the line of vast historical forces moving irresistibly to a goal. That this conviction is an effective one for good or ill is proved by the immense advance of Communism in our time.

In both these contemporary movements we observe that the driving force is not simply the idea as such, but the persuasion that the idea embodies itself in history as a concrete, living process. The Marxist, like the Nazi, is persuaded that he knows what the historical process is 'up to'. In his communist 'cell', like the Nazi in his 'storm-troop', he feels himself to be in the place where history is being made, and he makes it—to whatever ultimate effect.

It can scarcely be said that the 'Western democracies' have anything comparable.[1] They have some vaguely conceived principles on the one hand, and on the other hand some clearly defined, immediate, practical objectives; but there is no general sense that these principles and objectives are of the essential stuff of history. Recently the veteran Italian philosopher Benedetto Croce has offered us a possible basis for an historical 'ideology' in his dictum that history is the history of liberty. But that remains on the academic level.

The fact is that in this country at least we cherish the deepest suspicion of all large historical generalizations. A recent historian, the late H. A. L. Fisher, summed up his view of history in these words: 'Men wiser and more learned than I have discerned in history a plot, a rhythm, a predetermined pattern. These harmonies are concealed from me. I can see only one emergency following upon another as wave follows upon wave; only one great fact, with respect to which, since it is unique, there can be no generalizations; only one safe rule for the historian: that he should recognize in the

[1] Perhaps the nearest thing to a democratic 'ideology' was the 'philosophic radicalism' of the nineteenth century, combined with the 'Whig' interpretation of history; but it has no contemporary significance.

development of human destinies the play of the contingent and the unforeseen.'[1]

Such a view is undoubtedly congenial to our British temper. Did I say we had no 'ideology'? Possibly the interpretation of history as 'one emergency following upon another' is in fact the 'ideology' corresponding to our favourite practice of 'muddling through'—sometimes dignified by the name of 'practical opportunism'.

But I do not believe we can afford to leave the matter there. In these last years history has burst into our private lives with devastating effect. The violence of the impact is bewildering to anyone who does not understand that the forces of contemporary history have behind them the accumulated weight of a long past, which we can no longer ignore. There is no escape. It is now clear to every thinking man that his own life and death depend on historical factors operating on the large scale.

The problem of history has become the most urgent problem of our time. We stand at the end of an era. How are our lives to be directed so that the new shape of things may be a worth-while enterprise of the spirit of man, and not a drift or a collapse? What is the meaning that history holds, to which our lives are to conform? The 'ideologies' give their answers; for Marxism and National Socialism alike are interpretations of history which seek to give significance to contemporary life. I believe that we have in the Bible an interpretation of history which goes deeper than either, and comprehends important and relevant facts which both of them ignore. How then does the biblical view of history interpret our contemporary situation?

In order to help us to put the question rightly—for in any field of thought, to put the question rightly is to go a long way towards the right answer—I shall start from a recent

1 *History of Europe*, preface, p. v.

work which discusses the problem of history with exceptional breadth and penetration: Professor Arnold Toynbee's monumental *Study of History*, of which six volumes out of a probable ten have so far appeared.

Professor Toynbee starts with the fact of civilization as a given and observable phenomenon. Under the general concept are included some nineteen distinct civilizations—ranging, literally, 'from China to Peru', and going back to the earliest ages of which we have any knowledge. He first poses the question, How is the rise of civilization—or concretely, of civilizations—to be accounted for? and he works towards an answer by an inductive study of the rise of various civilizations so far as they are known to us.

He reviews several possible causes which have been alleged by various thinkers as sufficient to account for the phenomena. He concludes that the geographical and biological factors comprehended under the headings of 'race' and 'environment', though important, do not in themselves disclose a sufficient cause for the process by which civilizations arose. The process itself he shows to have had in each case the form of 'challenge and response'. The challenge may be delivered through physical conditions of race and environment, but the degree and nature of the human response cannot be fully accounted for without in some way going behind these factors. He concludes that the process may best be represented in terms of 'an encounter between two superhuman personalities'. Such an encounter, he shows, is 'the plot of some of the greatest stories and dramas that the human imagination has conceived'. Among these he includes the Old Testament story of Paradise Lost, which is the story of an encounter between God and the devil, and the story of the Passion of Christ in the Gospels, which, he says, portrays 'a second encounter between the same antagonists'.[1] We are thus

1 *A Study of History*, vol. i, pp. 271–2.

referred to the Bible (among other literature) for a clue to the historical problem of the rise of civilization.

I now pass on to some observations of Professor Toynbee's on the decline of civilizations. These observations touch us closely; for after a detailed analysis of the causes and symptoms of the decline of numerous civilizations which have decayed, he shows that many of these symptoms are unmistakably present in our own civilization at the time of writing—which was before the outbreak of the late war. The inference is that our Western civilization is well advanced in the process of decline. I do not think that this conclusion can well be shaken. Certainly no argument against it can be based upon the fact that every year we are able to move faster from one point to another, and to destroy more human lives with less expenditure of time and trouble. Observe, however, that our author does not say, as many do say, that our civilization is 'doomed'.[1] His philosophy, unlike that of Spengler and others who have written about 'the decline of the West', is not determinist. The condition of decline is itself a challenge, to which it should be possible to find an appropriate response.

He asks, therefore, what lines of action are open to people who are aware of living in a declining civilization, such as our own. He distinguishes four possible principles on which action may be based, enumerating them under catch-titles as follows:[2]

1. 'Archaism.' By this he means that, in disgust of the sordid present, we may idealize the 'good old times', and aim at restoring them as a cure for our present ills. Thus Fascist Italy dreamed itself back to the Roman Empire, and Nazi Germany glorified the heroic age of the German race, before it was corrupted by the 'Jewish' doctrines of Christianity. Similarly there are some in this country who hanker after

1 *Op. cit.* vol. IV, pp. 7–39.
2 *Op. cit.* vol. VI, pp. 49–175.

the lost paradise of a mediaeval Merry England. If 'Archaism' is put into practice, it tends to develop into violent political reaction.

2. 'Futurism.' This is much the same thing as what is often called 'revolutionary Utopianism'. It means that disgust of the present breeds fantasies of an entirely new order, unrelated (except by sheer antagonism) to anything in the existing order, which must be swept away before Utopia can be realized. Put into practice, 'Futurism' leads to a revolution of destruction.

3. 'Detachment.' This means that those who feel that the time is out of joint simply throw up the sponge and contract out of all responsibility for a situation too far gone for mending. This withdrawal may take the most diverse forms, from an ignoble 'escapism' (for which our age has, significantly, invented such a rich apparatus) to a life of elegant or sublime contemplation (and again it is significant that mystical or pseudo-mystical cults have an astonishing vogue nowadays).[1] This principle is barren of action. Yet Toynbee holds that there may be (as there have been in the past) situations so desperate that the only thing a person with high standards can do is to withdraw from them, and that such detachment is then the necessary preliminary to effective action on the fourth principle, to which we now pass.

4. 'Transfiguration.' This means that instead of attempting to move from the unsatisfactory present into a fantastic Golden Age in past or future time, or withdrawing altogether into

---

[1] One of these cults happened to be in session at an English country house towards the end of August 1939. The session was abruptly terminated by a government notice to vacate the premises within twelve hours. The bewildered adepts came out into a strange world. They had had their thoughts so concentrated upon higher realities (one of them explained to me) that they had no idea that things had reached such a pass.

the timeless world of the mystics, we bring the total situation, as we ourselves partake in it, into a larger context, which gives it new meaning. Transfiguration does involve a movement of detachment, but this movement is now only one element in a complex rhythm of 'withdrawal and return'. 'This way', writes Professor Toynbee, 'of taking our departure from the City of Destruction is not an act of truancy; it is a "withdrawal according to plan"; and the plan...is not to save ourselves by escaping from a dangerous and painful mundane entanglement, but to seize the initiative in order, at our own peril, to save the City of Destruction from its doom.'[1]

The larger context through which our total situation may be transfigured is best conceived in terms of *Civitas Dei*, or the Kingdom of God, 'which is not in Time at all—either present, future or past—and which differs from all temporal mundane states in the radical way of being in a different spiritual dimension, but which, just by virtue of this difference of dimension, is able to penetrate our mundane life and, in penetrating, to transfigure it'.[2] The classical account of 'Transfiguration' he finds in the New Testament, which has for its theme the coming of the Kingdom of God, and he illustrates his thesis in detail both from the story in the Gospels and from the account of the Christian way of life as it appears all through.

Of these four possible responses, 'Archaism' and 'Futurism' are self-destructive, as Professor Toynbee argues from a wealth of instances. 'Detachment' by itself is self-stultifying. Only 'Transfiguration', with its rhythm of withdrawal and return, is creative. It issues in 'Palingenesia', or rebirth.

Thus far Professor Toynbee. This meagre paraphrase of a long, elaborate and richly documented argument can, of course, do no sort of justice to his thought, though I hope

1 *Op. cit.* vol. VI, p. 167.   2 *Op. cit.* vol. VI, p. 131.

it has not seriously misrepresented him. My object here, however, is not to expound or criticize the Toynbeian philosophy of history, but to secure a point of view from which to approach the theme of this chapter: the bearing of the Bible upon the historical problem of our time. Our question, it now appears, might be put in this way: How may a study of the Bible help us towards the 'transfiguration' of our present historical situation?

Certain broad principles for the interpretation of history we may set down at once.[1]

1. God is sovereign over history, which serves His will and works out His purpose. This is presupposed all through.

2. On the other hand, the Bible lends no support to any theory which demands that the course of history should be fixed beforehand.

This needs some consideration, because there is a widespread misconception that the prophetical books are a kind of glorified 'Old Moore's Almanac', plotting out the future in cryptograms. Ingenious persons devote time and trouble, which they might well have spent on cross-word puzzles, to the attempt to discover the 'key to prophecy', just as others try to predict coming events from the measurements of the Great Pyramid. All such attempts presuppose that the course of events is so fixed that the apparent influence of human choice is an illusion. It is impossible to attribute such a view to the biblical writers.

The prophets certainly did forecast coming events. What, then, did they intend by such forecasts? They were primarily concerned with the immediate situation which faced them. In this situation they distinguished two elements: the constant element, which was the purpose of God, and the variable element, which was human action. They insisted that God must be thought of as a perfectly self-consistent Being, whose

1 Cf. also chap. v, pp. 120–121.

action in history discloses the immutable principles of justice, mercy and truth. To enforce this view, they dwelt much upon the 'mighty works' of God in the past. They then applied the lessons of the past to the understanding of the present. In doing so, they frequently formed 'intelligent anticipations' of the immediate consequences of actions then in process.

It must be observed that such anticipations are *conditional* (whether the condition is expressed or not). Prophetic predictions in general fall within such a formula as '*Except ye repent*, ye shall all in like manner perish'[1]. In the tale of Jonah there is a vivid picture of a prophet's chagrin when his prediction fell through because people did repent.[2] It may have been drawn from life. A prophet may on occasion have forgotten that his forecasts were conditional, and imagined himself a soothsayer. But the true intention of prophetic predictions is not to unveil an inevitable future, but to alter the variable element in the present situation—the action of men—in relation to the constant element—the will of God—and so to alter the resultant situation.

Such predictions are ordinarily at short range. The prophets do not write imaginary history covering centuries of the future, like Mr Shaw in *Back to Methuselah*, or Mr Wells in his scientific and philosophical romances. Their interest in the remoter future is confined to the one certainty of the ultimate triumph of the purpose of God. This triumph they may exhibit in dramatic form—a gathering of nations in the Valley of Decision, or a Battle of Armageddon. But they have no interest in 'dim aeonian periods' which may intervene. By a characteristic 'foreshortening', the End is always 'round the corner'. The *certainty* of the divine Event is translated into *imminence* in time.

Thus the biblical interpretation of history conforms to H. A. L. Fisher's 'one safe rule for the historian: that he

1 Luke xiii. 5.   2 Jonah iii–iv.

should recognize in the development of human destinies the play of the contingent and the unforeseen'.

3. This is because the Bible contemplates man as morally responsible within the framework of the divine purpose. 'See, I have set before thee this day life and good, and death and evil. . . . Therefore choose!'[1] That the choice is real, and has real consequences in history, is a biblical postulate.

Thus the Bible, while it affirms with complete confidence that history fulfils the purpose of God, encourages a sober agnosticism about the actual unfolding of that purpose in the course of events.

If therefore we are looking to the Bible for guidance towards an understanding of our own place in history, we shall not expect anything in the way of prediction. We are not to know how things are going to turn out. There is no promise of security, or plenty, or peace in our time, or the victory of this programme or that; any more than there is certainty that the 'end of the world', or of our civilization, is inevitably impending. 'It is not for you to know times or seasons, which the Father hath set within His own authority.'[2]

But what we may learn is the meaning of our present situation; that is, what God is saying to us in it. We have recognized in the Bible a passage of history punctuated by a series of crises in which the Word of God came to men, and visibly altered the course of events. Through this series of crises a meaning gradually emerged, which made sense of the whole. This meaning was ultimately clarified and confirmed by a final event in which 'the Word was made flesh', that is, was completely embodied in a Person and in His relations with the total historical situation. Looking backwards, we can see in the earlier crises 'foreshadowings' of

1 Deuteronomy xxx. 15, 19.
2 Acts i. 7.

the final event, in the sense that the emergent meaning was partially expressed in them, to be 'fulfilled' when the climax of the series was reached. In a somewhat similar sense, subsequent crises in history, including that of our own time, may be seen as 'after-shadowings' of the crisis provoked and shaped by the coming of Jesus Christ in the first century. So regarded, the events of our time will fall within the series in which the Word of God is spoken to men, and they will disclose their meaning to us. There are whole tracts of history which seem to us to be almost entirely meaningless. It is a possibility which cannot be excluded that the events of our time may end in a similar meaningless chaos. Even so, we may continue to trust that divine providence is over all history—as the author of the Book of Daniel believed that 'the Most High ruleth in the kingdom of men',[1] at a time when all the facts seemed against such a belief. But historically the belief established itself only where a sufficient number of those who participated in the course of events heard God speaking in it and responded.[2] Only upon the same terms is history likely to disclose its meaning to us now.

How then are we to read the Word of God in the complex realities of our present situation? I would not for a moment suggest that a faith instructed by the Bible is any substitute for a knowledge of the facts of economics, politics, history, psychology and the natural sciences which enter into the total situation—in any case as much of such knowledge as we can get. There is no substitute for honest thinking about the facts. But the specious facts (of the order I have indicated) do not exhaust the total reality with which we have to deal. The impact of these facts upon our minds, with the resultant

1 Daniel iv. 17, 25.
2 A 'sufficient number' in this sense may be a small minority. In Israel in the eighth century B.C. it was a mere 'remnant'; in the first century A.D. it was even smaller. But it sufficed.

meaning they bear for us, depends upon our response to more fundamental realities which are intermingled with the ostensible factors (of politics, economics and the rest) but are never fully covered by them. It is to our apprehension of these deeper realities that the Bible speaks.

We may best discover what it says about the present crisis in history by trying to trace in our present situation the pattern which we have discerned in the creative crises of the past, and particularly in the crisis of the Gospels. For the Word of God, while it is adapted to different historical levels, and did not come in exactly the same terms to Abraham and Moses, to Jeremiah and to the first Christians, is nevertheless found always to conform to one general pattern. In this pattern we have distinguished two complementary aspects; one negative, the other positive.

1. The impact of the Word of God upon an historical situation, as represented in the Bible, has, first, the negative effect of denying false values expressed in the situation as it has developed historically. The biblical term for this negative effect is 'judgement'. Judgement is often embodied outwardly in the form of historical disasters, which are the consequences of wrong attitudes, policies and actions. No doubt such disasters always have causes which can be expressed in terms of biological, political, or economic factors. But the Bible isolates for emphasis the factor of *morale*, in the largest sense.

Take for example the story of the Fall of the Kingdom of Judah before the advance of Babylon. It could be told as the tragic last stand of a little nation, foredoomed by its geographical position, slowly ground down under the pressure of two great empires, and finally brought to utter ruin by superior military strength. But as the long-drawn struggle emerges from the pages of prophecy, it discloses a squalid collapse of *morale*, the issue of a spiritual process of degeneration. This degeneration came about through repeated refusals of a moral challenge offered by the prophets. That is the central motive of the story. The disastrous events of the Babylonian conquest appear as a dramatization of the deeper disaster of spiritual and moral collapse. This is the manner of God's Word of judgement. It is a denial of the values which people had pursued in opposition to the truth as it was set before them.

Still clearer is the manner of divine judgement in the story of the crucifixion of Jesus Christ, which is the theme of the Gospels. It has sometimes been told in modern times as an episode in the struggle between Roman imperialism and Jewish nationalism; or between the cosmopolitan, secular 'ideology' of Graeco-Roman civilization and the religious isolationism of the Jews. It has been told, alternatively, as an episode in the emergence of the 'proletariate' of ancient society and its collision with the ruling class. If some such interpretation is adopted, then the various actors in the tragedy may claim more or less justification for their actions. So indeed they can, upon that level; for there is a real measure of truth in such renderings of the story. But confronted with the Gospels, these interpretations are seen to be superficial. The central issue is Jesus Christ's offer of a moral challenge, and its refusal by His contemporaries. That is why the story comes to have the aspect of a judgement-scene,[1] in which sentence is passed upon a series of typical figures, not unlike ourselves. It is passed, not chiefly in words, but by the part which individuals take in the action of the drama. The moral choices made by Pilate, Caiaphas and the priests, the scribes and Pharisees, the mob, Judas the traitor and the well-meaning but unstable disciples, are quite clear-cut, and are seen to be organically related to the tragic *dénouement*. History pillories them.

1 See p. 93.

Thus an approach from the biblical standpoint to our present situation will discern in it the factor of *morale* in the largest sense. Outwardly, we face the collapse of the social order over a large part of what was the civilized world—a collapse which involves all of us more or less. Inwardly, it is the collapse of the moral standards of Christendom. Just as in Israel spiritual decline was intimately related to persistent recalcitrance to the moral and spiritual ideals of the prophets, so our generation has suffered from appreciating high ideals and then denying them in practice. Probably there has never been a period when moral idealism in the political sphere touched a higher level, or commanded more intelligence in planning, or achieved more effective publicity. Yet the events—or in other words the corporate actions and reactions of the European nations—have denied such ideal values with a disastrous thoroughness. It seems to be a rule that ideals once enunciated, and accepted on the level of sentiment, become destructive if they are not put into action. To have seen the better and embraced the worse does not leave one in the same position as at first; it means moral decline; and that is the story of the European community in recent times. No doubt other explanations of our calamities may be adduced, with some measure of truth in most of them. But in comparison with the biblical explanation they are superficial. Fundamentally, the meaning of our present predicament is God's judgement upon our way of life.

History has been defined as a record of the crimes, vices and follies of mankind. We are in no position to quarrel with the definition. But if there is no more to be said, then history remains a meaningless chaos. If, however, it is clear that God, who stands above history, and yet communicates with us in history, passes judgement upon the situation, then there is introduced into the chaos an element of moral valuation. It makes us *responsible*, and to accept responsibility is the first step to a cure.

To accept responsibility, I say. It is easy to put responsibility upon other people: to stage trials of our former enemies, or to condemn them in our own minds. But that is not to take the matter with full seriousness. We shall get at the truth of our present situation only by exposing *ourselves* to the judgement of God in it.[1] A clear-sighted self-criticism is called for. I am not referring to the practice of self-examination, or introspection, as it is commonly recommended: a practice which is often extremely salutary and may also be harmful. I mean an effort to recognize our own behaviour as contributory to the corporate actions and reactions which have brought us to this pass, and to assess it by given moral standards.

For the standards are *given*, not thought up out of our own minds (always exposed as they are to prejudice in our own cause). In the Old Testament the prophets do not simply denounce the conduct of their people. They define with precision the particular tendencies in corporate life which are leading to disaster, because they are an affront to the Law of God—to the principles upon which the moral structure of the universe rests. These definitions are a series of shots, all hitting the target, and coming nearer and nearer to the centre. The New Testament finally hits the mark. An intelligent reading of the Gospels leaves us in no possible doubt what are the precise values which lie under condemnation as having a direct relation to the catastrophe of the crucifixion. It requires no inordinate effort of the imagination to see ourselves in the place of Pilate, Caiaphas, the Pharisees, the mob, the traitor and the unfaithful disciples; and such an effort is an effective way towards self-criticism of the kind which is

1 Upon the analogy of Amos i–ii, cf. I Peter iv. 17; see pp. 39–40, 107.

most relevant. I will leave it at that, only observing that the severest condemnation falls, paradoxically enough, upon those who, as individuals, were probably the most virtuous and intelligent of the lot: those who 'trusted in themselves that they were righteous and despised others'.[1]

2. We turn from the negative to the positive. Beyond judgement lies renewal. Indeed judgement, as we have seen, is properly no more than a secondary effect of the Word of God, which in its first intention is creative. In God the highest degree of creativity is combined with the highest degree of benevolence, or goodwill, towards all His creatures. Encountering evil in human life, His Word necessarily reacts in judgement; but not as though that were the goal of His intervention in the process. The evil once recognized and judged becomes a point of departure for some new and original kind of good. Consequently, it is just when all seems irreparably lost that the renewing power of God makes itself felt. The hopeless calamity of the crucifixion was reversed in the resurrection of Christ; as when Israel was completely broken, and not only broken but discredited, a new stage in its history began, like a resurrection from the dead. God 'calls the things that are not as if they were',[2] and always in the service of an endless goodwill.

This is what is meant by the forgiveness of sins. Forgiveness is not simply a device for easing the burdened conscience (though it has that effect). It is more like 'an inexhaustible capacity for new growth, embedded in the plastic foundations of the universe'.[3] Or rather, it is a creative act of the living God, which does not simply pass over the wreckage of past failures, but transforms and utilizes it. If we may put it so,

---

1 Luke xviii. 9.   2 Romans iv. 17.
3 I owe this quotation, if my memory serves me aright, to Mr Winston Churchill—I mean, of course, the other Winston Churchill, the American novelist.

the very wickedness of men gives God a new chance of creation. (That is why evil is bound to be overcome in the end, because its worst efforts call forth a more than countervailing power creative of good.) Forgiveness, then, is the power for a fresh start at the moment of deepest despair, 'according to the energy of the might of His strength, which He put into effect in Christ when He raised Him from the dead'.[1] Nor is it a purely individual matter, though it becomes real in becoming personal. It is an active force in history.

In our present situation, therefore, we have this ground of hope: that over and above all the ostensible factors at work there is an overruling factor which is the creative goodwill of God; and to this we cannot assign any necessary limits. When we survey the immanent possibilities of the situation, we must confess that the outlook is not promising. Much is said about the 'new world' for which we must plan, but the genuinely new factors upon which any plan must depend are not obvious. The more clear-sighted speak with a notable lack of assurance about what lies ahead. But we are not confined to the immanent possibilities of the situation. There is a further possibility; that creative energies from beyond history may enter into it and alter the whole prospect. God creates by His Word,[2] 'calling the things that are not as if they were'. In our present crisis, it may be, He is calling to something which does not yet exist in us, but will come into existence at His Word.

Here is something that we cannot plan. The initiative lies with God, who is speaking in the circumstances of our time to those who can hear. His Word awaits a response. The only admissible response from man to his Maker is obedience. The line of behaviour called for by obedience to God in the

1 Ephesians i. 19–20. Paul puts in every word he can think of that means effectual power.

2 For the implications of this, see chap. v, pp. 104–106.

present circumstances, in its particulars, is left to our conscience, fortified by all the knowledge of relevant facts that
we can get, and by honest thinking about them. But our
thinking must be directed, and our conscience informed,
upon principles which are given in God's self-revelation in
Christ, and in the relation between God and man there set
up. The Gospels are our guide.

To take one particular example, consider the significance
of the Gospel precepts about forgiveness for the historical
problem of our time. If our one ground of hope is God's
forgiveness of the evil resident in the present situation,[1] then
it follows by inexorable logic that our response must include
forgiveness of our enemies. By forgiveness I do not mean a
warm sentimentality that muffles real wrongs. God's forgiveness, we have seen, is creative action for the renewal of
human life wasted by evil, in full view of the reality of the
evil, but with steady goodwill towards those who have done
the evil. Human forgiveness is an attempt to imitate the
divine, within our human limitations. That is, it is constructive action, based upon persistent goodwill, and directed
towards 'overcoming evil with good'.[2] It is difficult, but it
need not be either complicated or abstruse. 'If thine enemy
hunger, feed him'[3] is not a bad beginning. However difficult,
the demand is clear. 'If you do not forgive men, neither will
your Father forgive your misdeeds.'[4] This is no arbitrary
ruling. It lies in the nature of the case. The creative goodwill
of God, which means the possibility of a fresh start out of
this fearful mess, becomes effective as it meets with the right
response from men and finds expression in their action.

Here then is the basis of the 'transfiguration' of the situation which is called for by the present crisis. It is, let me repeat,
a real concrete possibility here and now. The place where

1 See pp. 45–48, 53, 95.   2 Romans xii. 21.
3 Romans xii. 20.   4 Matthew vi. 15.

history is made is the place of encounter between God and man, where the Word of God is heard and man responds in obedience. Such is the purport of the whole biblical history. That history is alive in the Church, which was brought into being by it, and continually witnesses to it. In our time history is being made in the Church.

Not many years ago such a statement would have been met with a smile of incredulity. At this moment anyone who should dismiss the claim out of hand would show himself ignorant of what has been happening during the dark years all over Europe. The Church has been in many countries the sole effective custodian of values that were in danger of perishing from the earth. Divided as it is, the Church has spoken with one voice upon certain ultimate principles, whether the voice was that of an Orthodox metropolitan of Athens, a cardinal archbishop of Munich, or a Lutheran primate of Norway; an Anglican archbishop or a Roman Pope—or of many less conspicuous but not less faithful witnesses, some of whom paid dearly for their witness. There was no other voice that spoke with the like clarity and consistency.

Not only so, there was, in many countries, no other available centre for a community-life independent of perverted 'ideologies', and having promise for the future; and this corporate life expressed itself in common action. Most people know something of the part played in Norway by Bishop Berggrav and his clergy, and the school-teachers who followed his lead. In Holland the Church inflexibly resisted orders of the usurping government which were contrary to the Law of God. In France an unheard-of unity of witness between catholics and protestants gave inspiration to a bewildered people. In Germany there was a similar agreement of the two communions, unprecedented since the Reformation, in protest against iniquities and in succour of the oppressed. Since the close of the war we have learnt unsuspected facts about the persistence and weight of the 'church-opposition' in Germany—the only effective opposition there was, by general admission, even though it largely failed of immediate results.[1]

Whether these and similar activities of the Church in many countries will lead (as they might well do) to a new orientation of affairs we do not yet know. But in such actions we see the biblical history coming alive, with its perpetually recurrent themes: the recognition and acceptance of a divine judgement upon our common sin; the acknowledgement of a power to re-make human life; and the characteristic response, after the pattern of Christ and His apostles: 'we ought to obey God rather than men'.[2] We have, therefore, grounds for believing that history is being made in the Church. If so, it is not because the Church has a superior plan for reconstruction; or because its clergy speak with authority upon political or economic questions; or because its members are exceptionally virtuous or intelligent. It is because the Church, however low it falls, bears the indelible marks of its origin. It cannot help itself. It is bound to repeat in its services words and actions which recall the great divine Event out of which it arose;[3] and these have proved their power, even in its worst periods, to shake men with the sense that they are confronted by God in His judgement and His mercy, and to drive them to a decision.

Through seeing the process at work in a concrete institution we understand how contemporary history falls into the context of the history which is revelation. We have been too 'subjective' and individualist in our understanding of the

1 Recently it has been reported that a representative body of the German Evangelical Church has made a courageous statement acknowledging not only Germany's guilt, but also the Church's own share in that guilt, despite its efforts and its loyal witness to the truth.

2 Acts v. 29. 3 On this, see further, chap. VII, pp. 159–162.

Christian faith. The Bible deals all through with the conception of a *people* of God, which is the point of application of God's creative Word, and the place where history is made through man's response to it. Read in the light of that conception, and in the context of an actual community playing its part in the drama of our time, it becomes acutely relevant to our contemporary problem.

CHAPTER VII

HISTORY AND THE INDIVIDUAL

THE title of this chapter suggests a problem which we are bound to raise at this stage of our study. We have surveyed the biblical literature as a record of many centuries of history. Now history consists of *public* events, events which have significance for whole communities, and in the last resort for the entire human race. The biblical history is in this sense public. It forms part of the history of mankind. It is a *fait accompli*, standing there, unalterable. In this biblical history we are to find a revelation of God, in a sense which I have tried to explain. I have also tried to show that it can be so understood as to give meaning to history in our own time.

All through I have deliberately laid emphasis upon this public, 'objective' character of the biblical revelation. Yet the human race, and all historical communities, consist of individual selves. Each of us has responsibilities to bear, and decisions to make, which go to the shaping of an individual character, personality, and destiny. However our lives may be knit up with society, the point comes at which we must stand alone—unless God is with us. God, we say, has given a public, historical revelation of Himself in the Bible. But it cannot be effectively a revelation *for us*, unless that which is public becomes private; unless history becomes personal to ourselves. There lies our problem. Where is the passage from the Bible as public history to the Bible as a personal revelation of God to those who seek Him?

There is a strong temptation to short-circuit this problem by suggesting that the historical study of the Bible is something quite apart from its 'devotional' study. 'All these critical and historical questions' (some would say) 'no doubt have their place and their importance for the specialist, but for personal religion they do not matter. You may leave them aside. It is the immediate suggestiveness of the Bible to your mind and heart that will be of benefit to you. That is how God speaks to you.'

It is certainly true that the historical study of the Bible has sometimes worn the appearance of a cold-blooded anti-quarianism, with no obvious relevance to the spiritual needs of the individual. It is also true that it belongs to all great literature, and not least to the Bible, to evoke in the mind of the reader meanings and associations which may have nothing to do with the circumstances of its origin, or the intentions of its writers, and yet may bring genuine illumination and enrichment to the mind. A literature which draws from such profound depths as the Bible does cannot but possess this sug-gestive or evocative power in a high degree. We shall have to lay ourselves open to it, by meditation and a receptive patience, if we are to receive what the Bible is designed to give us. But that is not all. There are other great religious books which possess this power. I am told that in some churches you may be served with Selections from Great Authors in place of readings from the Scriptures. I have no doubt that they stir devout feelings and high aspirations. But these 'subjective' moods are not the same thing as God's revelation of Himself to us.

The Bible differs from other religious literature in that it stakes everything upon the assumption that God really did reveal Himself in particular, recorded, public events. Unless we take this assumption seriously, the Bible hardly makes sense as a whole, whatever spiritual stimulus we may receive from selected portions. The facts of history—that is, the things that happened, with the meanings they bore for those who experienced them—are something *given*. Whatever response the words of Scripture may evoke in our minds, through meditation and waiting upon the truth, must submit to control by the facts. Otherwise we are in danger of taking 'autosuggestion' for the Word of God, and missing something that might tear to pieces the fantasies we have woven, and tell us truths about ourselves that we never suspected. Consequently there ought to be no separation between the 'historical' and the 'devotional' study of the Bible.

The question, however, remains, how we are to bridge the gap between history and the experience of the individual. Let us turn again to the Bible itself for an approach to the answer.

We have already observed that at a certain point in the Old Testament there is a change of emphasis.[1] In the earlier parts the emphasis is upon the community; in the later parts the individual is more directly in view. The change is pretty clearly marked by the work of Jeremiah, especially his conception of a 'new covenant' under which the Law of God is to be 'written on the heart', and every individual for himself is to 'know the Lord'. Jeremiah's successor, Ezekiel, as we saw, emphasizes the moral responsibility of the individual almost to exaggeration. In the characteristic literature of the period after the return from Exile, the individual note is well marked, if not predominant. The Books of Proverbs and Ecclesiasticus are in large part manuals of individual conduct and piety. The Book of Job deals with the problem of undeserved suffering, no longer in terms of national calamity, but entirely from the point of view of the individual. Ecclesiastes is haunted by the apparent futility of life as it is experienced by individual men and women. The Psalms are a treasury of personal devotion. It is in this period, and notably in the 'apocalyptic' literature beginning with the

1 See chap. III, pp. 45–48.

Book of Daniel, that the idea of personal immortality begins to play a significant part; and this in itself attests a new value attached to the individual.

In some sense this later literature, subsequent to the extinction of the kingdom of Judah, represents the entry of the individual into the field of religion. We might compare with it the way in which in Greek history the individual came into his own after the old city states lost their freedom and importance.

This change of emphasis was made much of by an influential school of writers and preachers in the recent past. It was obviously congenial to the highly individualist climate of the nineteenth century. How welcome was the discovery that the 'progressive revelation' in the Bible led away from a primitive collectivism to an enlightened individualism! But the change was certainly exaggerated. The case is not so simple.

In particular, it would be untrue and misleading to suggest that the New Testament represents the culmination of a development in the direction of individualism. It is of course true that the religious and moral significance of the individual is asserted by New Testament writers at least as firmly as by Jeremiah; but on the other hand the conception of an organic solidarity of the people of God reaches its fullest expression in the New Testament idea of the Church as the 'Body of Christ'.[1]

The comparison, which I suggested above, with the development of Greek thought aptly illustrates the point. There is no mistaking the thoroughgoing individualism of the Hellenistic world in the New Testament period. It found its highest expression in the Stoic philosophy, which, for all its efforts to call men to the service of humanity, had for its aim the 'self-sufficiency' of the individual (his 'autarky', as the

1 See pp. 72–73.

10-2

newspapers now say, adopting a word from the vocabulary of Stoicism, but usually misspelling it). In contrast, anyone can see that Christianity brought into that world a new idea, and practice, of community.

But even in the Old Testament the break which we have noted at the time of Jeremiah is not nearly so complete as might appear on the surface. All through the Bible the individual is contemplated in the context of the community, though the emphasis shifts to some extent. In Jeremiah and his followers the individual acquires new significance, but the sense of the solidarity of the people of God persists, and comes into full view again in the New Testament. On the other hand, the rôle of the individual is more significant in the earlier literature than has sometimes been recognized.

Let us examine the literature again, from this point of view. The earlier books in general certainly betray a very vivid sense of the solidarity of the nation, so much so that the community can be addressed, or spoken of, as if it were one person 'Israel is my son, my firstborn', says the Book of Exodus.[1] 'I taught Ephraim to walk', says Hosea.[2] God is Father of the nation rather than of the individual Israelite. In the precepts of the Law and the prophets alike the second person singular 'thou shalt' alternates with the second person plural 'ye shall' in a way which often makes it difficult to say whether 'thou' means the people as a 'corporate personality', or the individual member of the community considered with regard to his station in the religious society.

There are long passages where the history of the people through a whole period is told as if it were the biography of an individual.

Thou shalt remember all the way which the Lord thy God hath led thee these forty years in the wilderness. . . . Thy

1 Exodus iv. 22.　　　　　　2 Hosea xi. 3.

raiment waxed not old upon thee, neither did thy foot swell, these forty years.[1]

Is it the individual Israelite who wore one suit of clothes for forty years, and avoided footsoreness during a long trek? Or is this a way of saying that the nation passed through a period of nomadic existence without sustaining damage? Read the whole of the eighth chapter of Deuteronomy and decide.

Again, it is held by many critics, with great probability, that some of the stories of the patriarchs are actually accounts of the movements and actions of whole tribes, given as if they were adventures of individual persons. In the Book of Judges we read:

Judah said unto Simeon his brother, Come up with me into my lot, that we may fight against the Canaanites, and I likewise will go with thee into thy lot. So Simeon went with him. And Judah went up, and the Lord delivered the Canaanites and the Perizzites into their hand.[2]

Pretty clearly that means that there was an alliance between the *tribes* of Judah and Simeon against the neighbouring tribes of Palestine.[3] Thus far the Book of Judges. But in Genesis xxxiv we have a circumstantial narrative according to which 'two of the sons of Jacob, Simeon and Levi', slew 'Hamor and Shechem his son', in revenge for an insult to their 'sister' Dinah. Does that mean that the tribes of Simeon and Levi in alliance sacked the city of Shechem, in

1 Deuteronomy viii. 2, 4. There is an extraordinary passage in Ezekiel xvi, where the history of Israel is told in the form of a romantic tale about a foundling child who was adopted into a rich family and then went to the bad.

2 Judges i. 3–4.

3 The sons of Jacob, according to the chronology of the Old Testament, belong to a period at least 400 years before the conquest of Canaan.

revenge for an attack upon a kindred tribe called Dinah? It seems quite plausible. If we are unable to decide the question dogmatically, that in itself shows how unstable, at this stage of Hebrew thought, was the distinction between individual and corporate personality.

And yet, during the period when the sense of community seems at times to eclipse the individual, outstanding personalities count. It is not only that the earlier prophets whose writings we possess—Amos, Hosea, Isaiah—have as strongly marked individuality as any of their successors. Before their time, right back to the 'heroic age', the course of history often turns upon the influence of great men, rooted always in their personal relations with God.[1] Their exploits may at times have been magnified by legend, but the very fact that legends gathered about them is proof of their outstanding influence.[2] The Exodus from Egypt may have been in one sense a mass-movement, but it is impossible to mistake the extent to which it depended upon Moses, with his conviction of a divine call. Even in the dim patriarchal age, while it may be true that some of the narratives really refer to tribal movements, there are others which lay all the stress upon religious experience of a strongly individual kind. The strange legend of the destruction of the Cities of the Plain has its vital centre in Abraham's encounter with God. 'Behold now, I have taken upon me to speak unto the Lord, which am but dust and ashes.... Shall not the Judge of all the earth do right?'[3] It might come out of the Book of Job, though it was written many centuries earlier. The story of Jacob's wrestling at the ford with a nameless Adversary[4] is primitive, almost barbaric;

1 The Epistle to the Hebrews (ch. xi) reviews the whole course of Hebrew history in terms of a succession of 'heroes of faith', and this is not untrue to the spirit of the Old Testament.

2 See pp. 54–55. 3 Genesis xviii. 22–33.
4 Genesis xxxii. 24–31.

but it convincingly represents the loneliness of the human
soul at grips with the unseen Powers.

Clearly it would be over-simplifying the facts to say that
the pre-exilic period is the age of corporate religion and the
post-exilic period the age of personal religion. And we may
suspect that the curious hesitation between individual and
corporate personality is something more than a weakness of
early Hebrew thought. This is confirmed when we find it
apparently recurring in one of the most profound of all the
biblical writers, the so-called 'Second Isaiah', whose work
closes the classical period of prophecy.[1]

His prophecies are dominated by the conception of the
'Servant of the Lord', a figure embodying the ideal of
absolute devotion to God in service, suffering and sacrifice.
If we ask whether the Servant is an individual or a group
or the nation as a whole, we shall find apparently contradictory
answers.[2] We can only conclude that in the mind of this
prophet the nation is worthy to be called God's servant only
when it is so entirely united in devotion to Him that it
renders Him service as one man; and no man, however great
and wise and good, is God's servant in the fullest sense unless
he transcends his individual self and lives in and for his people
in the service of their God. We can recognize an approach
to this ideal in several of the great figures of the Old Testament. Christian instinct has not been at fault in looking for
its complete fulfilment to Jesus Christ. But in itself the idea
of the Servant of the Lord throws light upon the peculiar
interpenetration of individual and corporate conceptions of
religion in the Bible.

We now turn to the later portions of the Old Testament.
Here the emphasis, as we have seen, falls largely upon the
individual aspect of religion. There are however in this

1 See chap. III, pp. 49–50.
2 See, e.g., Isaiah xli. 8, xlii. 6–7, 18–19, xliii. 10, xlix. 1–6.

period no more of those outstanding personalities who domi-
nate the earlier scene. The prophets after the Exile are of a
lesser breed, and most of the authors of the period are anonymous members of the community who give expression to a
wide range of religious experience as it comes to individuals
living within the framework of a religious society.

This is especially true of the Psalms.[1] No attentive reader of
this collection of religious poetry can fail to notice how much
of it is written in the first person singular. If, however, we
reflect, it is not always clear who this 'I' may be. Com-
mentators often discuss the question whether the 'I', in a
given passage, is really the individual poet, or whether he is
speaking for a group or for the people as a whole. Let us
take some examples:

> Hear my prayer, O Lord,
>> And let my cry come unto thee....
> My heart is smitten like grass, and withered;
>> For I forget to eat my bread.
> By reason of the voice of my groaning
>> My bones cleave to my flesh...
> I wake and am become
>> Like a sparrow that is alone upon the housetop...
> My days are like a shadow that declineth,
>> And I am withered like grass.[2]

The poet, it appears, is suffering from a wasting sickness.
He has no appetite; he lies awake at night; he is losing flesh.
In his trouble he turns to God:

1 If a considerable number of Psalms go back to the prophetic
period or earlier, as some modern critics hold (in opposition to the
view which prevailed thirty years ago), then there is additional
support for the view that there was no such radical change from
collective to individual conceptions at the Exile as has often been
asserted. But the Psalter seems to be substantially post-exilic.

2 Psalm cii. 1, 4–5, 7, 11.

But thou, O Lord, shalt abide for ever;
    And thy memorial unto all generations.
Thou shalt arise and have mercy upon Zion;
    For it is time to have mercy upon her;
      Yea, the set time is come. . . .
For the Lord hath built up Zion,
    He hath appeared in his glory. . .
That men may declare the name of the Lord in Zion,
    And his praise in Jerusalem;
When the peoples are gathered together,
    And the kingdoms, to serve the Lord.[1]

There is not a word here of the poet's recovery from sickness. It is all about God's deliverance of His people and the coming of His Kingdom. Then were we mistaken in supposing that the 'I' of the earlier verses was the individual poet, and is he really speaking all through of the troubles of Israel, under the figure of sickness?

Or consider the *De Profundis*:[2]

Out of the depths have I cried unto thee, O Lord;
    Lord, hear my voice.
Let thine ears be attentive
    To the voice of my supplications.
If thou, Lord, shouldest mark iniquities,
    O Lord, who shall stand?
But there is forgiveness with thee,
    That thou mayest be feared.
I wait for the Lord, my soul doth wait,
    And in his word do I hope.
My soul looketh for the Lord,
    More than watchmen wait for the morning;
    Yea, more than watchmen for the morning.

Could there be any more moving expression of personal dependence upon God? But the poet continues:

1 Psalm cii. 12–13, 16, 21–22.   2 Psalm cxxx.

> O Israel, hope in the Lord;
>   For with the Lord there is mercy,
>   And with him is plenteous redemption.
> And he shall redeem Israel
>   From all his iniquities.

Then is the Psalm after all a confession of *national* sins, and an appeal for national deliverance?

Take, again, the greatest of the so-called 'penitential Psalms', the fifty-first—the classical expression, in all literature, of a soul burdened with a sense of sin. It should be read as a whole. Nothing, it seems, could be more deeply individual—

> Behold, I was shapen in iniquity
>   And in sin did my mother conceive me[1]—

Yet it leads up to the petition,

> Do good in thy good pleasure unto Zion,
>   Build thou the walls of Jerusalem.[2]

Should we then conclude that the 'I' of the Psalm is really the nation corporately, repentant of its unfaithfulness to God's covenant, and pleading for restoration?

It is surely clear that first impressions are not to be trusted to give us a firm answer to the question whether the piety of the Psalms is individual or corporate. The twenty-third Psalm ('The Lord is my shepherd') can be read all through as a confession of God's care for the individual, but it cannot properly be separated from the eightieth ('Give ear, O Shepherd of Israel'), and many other passages which speak of the people collectively as God's flock. Again, Psalm cvi is a poetical survey of the history of Israel from the Exodus to the Babylonian captivity; yet its interest is not purely historical, for the poet prays 'Remember me, O Lord, with

---

1 Psalm li. 5.   2 Psalm li. 18.

the favour that thou bearest unto thy people' (v. 4). He is laying claim to his birthright as a member of God's people, and wishes to experience for himself the mercy of God as it is exhibited in the history of Israel.

Here is a clue to the real character of this religious poetry. The Psalmists are not outstanding personalities, like prophets and leaders of the past, who out of the exceptional depth of their own experience initiated great movements in history. They are lay members of the community, who share intimately in its corporate memories and hopes. God's dealings with His people in history enter into their own souls. For them public facts have become private experience. As members of the people of God they are made free of all that the history of that people has revealed of the ways of God with men.[1]

Here we have again, from a somewhat different point of view, that interpenetration of individual and corporate elements in religion which we noted in the earlier literature. It is in fact typical of the Bible as a whole. It is clarified and placed on a reasoned basis in the New Testament doctrine of the Church.

The solidarity of the Church is set forth in expressive metaphors. The Church is a body. 'As we have many members in one body,' writes Paul, 'and all the members have not the same function, so we, who are many, are one body in Christ.'[2] Again, he compares the people of God to an olive-tree. Men and women are slips 'grafted' into the stock, and so are

[1] There is a traditional rule of the Church that the Psalms as used in worship should not be considered as expressing, directly, the experience of the individual worshipper, but referred to Christ and the Church, the individual entering into them as a member of the Church. In the light of what is said in the following pages, it is clear that this rule has an historical basis. It cannot readily be applied everywhere, but it goes a long way.

[2] Romans xii. 4–5.

nourished by its sap.[1] Similarly in the Gospel according to John, Christians are like the branches of a vine, drawing life from the parent stem.[2] The Vine is Christ, for the Church is what it is solely through dependence on Him. So, too, in Paul's metaphor of the body, Christ is the Head, and we the members.[3] Thus the individual's relation to Christ is given in his relation to the Church which is the Body of Christ. 'Christ loved the Church and gave Himself for it',[4] he writes, and also (and therefore) 'He loved me and gave Himself for me'.[5] The one Body is inhabited by one Spirit, which is the Spirit of Christ, and in consequence the gifts of the Spirit are imparted to each individual member 'in the inner man'.[6] On the other side, when a member of the Church has to suffer for the good cause, he can say 'I am making up what is lacking of Christ's sufferings on behalf of His body, which is the Church'.[7]

If now we recall that the Church, by virtue of its origin, is the heir of the whole history of God's dealings with His people, we are in a position to draw from the Bible itself a solution of the problem posed in this chapter. For its writers the public, 'objective', revelation of God in history is also a revelation of His ways with each of us. There is a famous passage in the *Republic* of Plato where the philosopher is discussing the nature of justice, or righteousness. We find ourselves in difficulties, he suggests, if we attempt to arrive at a definition directly from an analysis of the individual soul. But in the community, the difference between justice and injustice is written 'in large letters' which our myopic minds can read, and there we shall be able to recognize justice in the soul. We may borrow his image, and say that the Bible

---

1 Romans xi. 17.   2 John xv. 1–6.
3 Ephesians i. 22–23; cf. also I Corinthians xii. 12.
4 Ephesians v. 25.   5 Galatians ii. 20.
6 Ephesians iv. 1–7, iii. 16.   7 Colossians i. 24.

depicts God's ways with man in the 'large letters' of the history of a community. If we can spell them out, we shall read also His ways with us individually. It is a matter of 'living ourselves into' the biblical history, which is the story of Everyman—and therefore of each of us.

We read here how Everyman (and therefore you and I) was destined to wear the image and likeness of God, and how he has lost that likeness through egoism and disobedience ('Each of us has been the Adam of his own soul', said a Jewish writer[1]); how Everyman (you and I) is under God's Law, but refractory to that law; how he wanders in the wilderness seeking for a 'promised land'—and perhaps when he gets there finds it disappointing, and must still seek the 'city that hath foundations'.[2] We read how Everyman (you and I) is beset by hostile powers, against which he must strive on pain of extinction ('There is no discharge in that war').[3] He goes after false gods, and courts disaster; but out of the disaster, under the providence of God, comes the opportunity of a fresh start. As we look down the vista—whether of the history of the people of God or of our own lives—it ends with inevitable death and a tomb; but beyond the tomb lies Easter Day.

There is here a history which we can 'live ourselves into', and in doing so, find the meaning of our own lives. I do not say that there is a kind of foreordained correspondence between the events of individual lives and the events of history; though it is certainly true that the hidden creative forces that mould individual lives are essentially the same as those which have moulded the lives of peoples and of the human race. Some psychologists report that their deep analysis of the Ego leads them back to a 'racial unconscious'. But that is not the point here. What I suggest is, that that

1 Apocalypse of Baruch liv. 19. 2 Hebrews xi. 10.
3 Ecclesiastes viii. 8.

which gives *meaning* to the biblical history also gives meaning to our individual lives. The biblical history is meaningful, because of the interpretation of events supplied by the Word of God through prophetic men—an interpretation which, as we have seen, is itself creative of events. The same interpretation applied to our lives will make them meaningful also. This interpretation always rests upon an encounter with God. As the story comes alive in us, we too encounter God, and our lives gain meaning.

We seem here to have arrived at a principle upon which we may make the passage from the revelation of God in the public facts of history to our own personal experience. The question, however, may be raised, whether there is not something arbitrary and even fanciful in this attempt to recognize ourselves (for that is what it comes to) in this piece of very ancient history. Granted that God revealed Himself in it, the revelation was after all addressed to a particular people at a particular period under particular conditions. What right have we to appropriate it to ourselves?

To this I should reply, first, that the biblical writers themselves have deliberately indicated that the revelation addressed to Israel and to the primitive Church was intended for all mankind. Here we see the importance of what I have called the universalizing framework in which the whole story is set.[1] The story is about 'Adam', that is to say, Man. Every son of Adam, or in other words, every individual to whom the generic term 'man' applies, is concerned in it. The story culminates in a Last Judgement upon the quick and the dead, and of necessity we are all concerned in that. It is a logical corollary that in all that falls between these poles we each and all of us have a part.

While, however, the biblical history becomes in principle universal history through the framework in which it is set,

1 See pp. 112–119.

it achieved effective universality only in the emergence of the Church as a 'catholic' body. Here for the first time we find in history a genuinely universal society. It has no qualification for entrance except that a man should freely accept God's covenant upon God's own terms. In its membership racial, national and social differences are irrelevant. A man stands before God simply as a man, a son of Adam, sharing Adam's tragic fate, but entitled to a higher destiny in Christ, who is called the 'second Adam'[1]—the Representative of man under God's mercy as Adam represents him under God's judgement. This catholic Church is, as we have seen, the final historical form of the people of God. And the Church is still here.[2]

In the foregoing chapter I suggested that the Church (with all its imperfections on its head) is still in our time the place where history is being made, through the encounter of man with God. We may now ask whether we can learn, from the way the Church actually functions, anything which bears upon our present problem—how the individual is to appropriate as personal experience that which is given to us in the Scriptures.

Among all the multiple activities of the Church there are two particular actions in which its true nature and function are disclosed. Whatever else it may do (which perhaps it ought not to have done), or leave undone (which perhaps it ought to have done), it declares the Gospel and it celebrates the Sacraments. Both are deeply rooted in the history out of which it emerged, and both have been characteristic of it in all periods of its existence.

The content of the Gospel as it was first proclaimed we have already studied.[3] The Church re-interprets it in terms

1 I Corinthians xv. 45–49; cf. Romans v. 18–19.
2 See the definition of the Church, quoted p. 4 note 5.
3 See pp. 74–79.

intelligible to successive periods, but its substance does not change. In declaring the Gospel, the Church recalls the great Event from which its own life began, and in doing so testifies out of a lengthening experience that this event really was a 'mighty act' of the living God, persisting in its consequences to this day. Like the first 'announcers' of the Gospel, it recognizes in this event the 'fulfilment' of the long-continued process by which the purpose of God worked in history. This is represented in the services of the Church by the regular reading of passages from the Old and New Testaments. These are read neither as 'elegant extracts', nor as merely historical information—least of all as 'pegs' upon which a preacher may hang ideas of his own. They are read as the record of the Word of God embodied in an historical process which, in the context of the life of the Church, becomes contemporary. In hymns and prayers and preaching the living voice of the Church responds, and adds its testimony to the Word. Those who hear, in the setting of the Church's corporate worship, are summoned, upon each particular occasion, to place themselves within the history which is God's revelation, at the point where it culminates in Jesus Christ, and to lay themselves open to the Word of judgement and of renewal which is spoken there to every human being.

The manner of it becomes clearer when we consider the sacraments of Baptism and the Eucharist (the Holy Communion or Lord's Supper, or, as it is called in some Western churches, the Mass). These are sometimes spoken of as 'sacraments of the Gospel'; rightly, because they express in dramatic action the realities which the Gospel expresses in words.[1]

1. In Baptism the individual is given, so to speak, the

1 In what follows, I am not attempting a 'doctrine of the Sacraments', but only calling attention to certain aspects of them which bear upon our present subject.

freedom of the city of God. He is incorporated in the historic community of God's people. The significance of the action is thus described by Paul:

All of us who were baptized into Christ Jesus were baptized into his death. We were therefore buried with Christ through baptism into a state of dea~~th~~ in order that, as Christ was raised from the dead thr~~ough~~ ~~th~~e glory of the Father, so we should walk in newness of ~~life~~.[1]

In other words, baptism signifies the re-enactment in the individual of the death and resurrection of Christ, in which the whole process of revelation in history came to a head. Let us recall that the Bible represents this fact of death-and-resurrection as giving the essential pattern of the entire history of man under the Word of God. When Abraham left Ur of the Chaldees, he was renouncing one kind of life in order to enter upon a new life on terms of God's covenant. When Israel went out of Egypt, they left a secure, though servile, way of life for the unknown perils and privations of the wilderness, in order that they might be fitted for new ways of life under God's Law. At the Babylonian conquest they died as an independent nation, with political and military ambitions, to rise again as a community dedicated wholly (in intention) to the service of religion. This is the pattern on which the purpose of God shaped the history of His people.[2] In baptism the same pattern is applied, through Christ, to the history of the individual.

2. The Eucharist is a sacrament which expresses our solidarity in the Body of Christ. 'We, who are many', says

---

1 Romans vi. 3–4.
2 As we have seen (p. 114) this pattern is given a mythical form in the story of the Deluge and the covenant with Noah; and this story is in Church tradition, going back to I Peter iii. 20–21, used as a symbol of Baptism.

Paul, 'are one body, because we all partake of the one bread.'[1] In performing this act of solidarity, we 'proclaim the Lord's death'.[2] We rehearse the Gospel story, which has its crucial point in the death-and-resurrection of Christ.[3] In most churches this act of 'remembrance' now takes the form of a comparatively brief and allusive summary recalling the essential facts. It was not always so. Some of the early liturgies of the Church contain a lengthy recital, summarizing not only the salient facts of the whole Gospel story, but also outstanding episodes of the Old Testament from the Creation onwards, and running to some pages in the service-book. I should not recommend the revival of this as a practical reform of our services; but the idea is perfectly sound. We 'remember' the Gospel facts in their total setting in the biblical history. Then, repeating what our Lord said and did on 'the night in which He was betrayed', we place ourselves within the history of our redemption at its crucial moment. It was there that the life of the Church began, and always begins anew. It is no longer past history. It is happening, and we are there. Then, by partaking in the Communion, we lay ourselves open individually to its whole meaning as the Word of God to us.

The Sacraments thus provide a pattern of the way in which the historical and corporate becomes individual and contemporary. I do not say that the Bible can speak to us effectively *only* within the Church. It would be rash to place any limits to its proved ability to appeal to men in the most varied circumstances, provided that they permit the impact of the biblical facts themselves upon the mind. But the Church is included among those facts.[4] Church and Bible

1 I Corinthians x. 17.
2 I Corinthians xi. 26.
3 See pp. 75–76, 89–96.
4 See chap. iv, pp. 70–73, 76–77.

are so closely bound together in one historical complex that it is only common sense to expect the Bible to speak to us most clearly in the context of the continuing life of the Church. If we are to 'live ourselves into' the history which is God's revelation of Himself to man, we have no need to take a flying leap into a remote and alien past. The Church is heir to that history and makes us free of it. What happens then lies between a man and his Maker.

INDEX OF REFERENCES

(165)

(167)